Through the Hole in My Head

Tom Taylor

With a thankful heart *Through the Hole in My Head* is dedicated to my wife, Nancey, my son Paul, my daughter Susan, who died in February 2000, and to all other members of my family for all that they have given to me.

08475006

ISBN 1 85852 167 X

Printed by Stanley L Hunt (Printers) Ltd, Rushden, Northants

Foreword

Shot in the head, left for dead, in the open under a blazing tropical sun without shelter from shellfire, alone except for the corpses of enemy soldiers and those of men who had been his comrades.

Without sustenance, solace of any kind, stripped of his uniform and equipment by marauding Japanese troops and cast aside while a battle raged around him for five days and four nights. In the afternoon of the fifth day the fighting came to an end and Corporal Tom Taylor of D Company, second Battalion, the Border Regiment, was found by some stretcher-bearers and carried to the Regimental Aid Post instead of to one of the shallow graves where 52 of his erstwhile comrades were being laid to rest . . . A man who knew him had thought he had seen the corporal move!

It was not without some trepidation that I was persuaded to include the foregoing incident in a book of war memoirs, which was published in 1973. I was among a mere handful of Border Regiment veterans who had witnessed the beginning and the end of Corporal Taylor's last battle in the war in Burma.

I had seen Tom shot down by enemy machine gun fire at about three o'clock in the afternoon of 31st January 1945. I had watched his sun-blackened emaciated body strapped to the stretcher of a jeep ambulance sometime in the afternoon of 4th February.

I had heard the medical officer telling me that Tom was alive – just! And wondered if that gallant soldier would survive, in his condition, the long jeep drive back to the Casualty Clearing Station. I doubt if those with me ever expected to see him again.

For more than 30 years I had been obsessed by thoughts of what it must have been like to experience the nightmare beyond imagining which Tom Taylor had endured.

At the Burma Star Reunion in London in 1976 I met the ex-stretcher-bearer Sergeant Eddie Hampson who had helped to carry Tom Taylor from no-man's land to the Regimental Aid Post all those years ago and he told me the following extraordinary twist of fate which lead the two old soldiers to meet again.

Eddie was in the congregation at Goose Green Methodist Church in Wigan on Sunday earlier that year when he had been introduced to the blind war veteran and guest speaker Tom Taylor.

Surely there must have been something beyond just plain guts and good luck – something supernatural, perhaps – which enabled Tom Taylor to hold on to life so tenaciously.

What he did with that life, with rare qualities of perception, intelligence, stubborn determination and literally, 'blind faith', he writes about in *Through the Hole in my Head*. It is a story which not only inspired me but humbled and uplifted me also.

Major Ken W Cooper
February 2001

Introduction

When I was 22 years old, I was shot in the head by a Japanese sniper's bullet as I led an infantry section into battle during the Burma Campaign of the second world war. The missile skimmed the vital sensory area of the brain, leaving me without the senses of sight, taste and smell. In spite of the loss of my eyesight and other faculties I would like to regard myself as a rational human being, and at 78 years of age still mentally and physically active in the social and religious life of the community.

My story begins just outside the village of Satpangan, close to the west bank of the river Irrawaddy in Burma, on the morning of 31st January 1945, and concludes in the Great Hall of Lancaster University on the 3rd December 1982. The chapters in between mark the progress from the moment the bullet struck my head until the award of my Master's degree.

There is a gap of over two months at the start of the drama, of which I am almost completely oblivious. This closed-off period of my life is put together by people who were there at the time, and who took part in the unfolding events. Details about my days in no man's land have gradually come to light in recent years, as I have met up with former colleagues.

Since my part in the war ended, I have had another fight, of a more subtle nature, to contend with – a battle for 'a place in the sun' – for independence, security, self-confidence and self-respect. Acquiring independence is a struggle for most blind people, and sometimes a losing one. I have to accept that I am not always as free as I once was, to do what I would like to do and to go where I would like to go at a time of my choosing. The simplest of tasks, which present no difficulty to an able-bodied child, can assume mammoth dimensions to anyone with visual difficulties. I have to recognise my limitations, but this said, it has not prevented me from living a serviceable life, exploiting to the full my remaining senses and faculties, and whatever resources have been available to me.

I cannot say that I have overcome all the obstacles single-handed. From the moment the bullet struck my head I have needed the services of many others to enable me to live a normal social life. I was not able even to pick myself up from the battlefield without the help of my rescuers, nor could I have nursed myself back to health and fitness without the professional care and treatment of neuro-surgeons and their competent nursing staff. Someone had to be there when I needed them – someone was there. It would have been impossible, too, to rehabilitate myself and to regain my self-respect, self-confidence and independence, without greater resources than I could muster on my own. These resources were available in the form of specialist agencies – St Dunstan's, The Royal Institute for the Blind, and other national and local organisations, with their wealth of experience in coping with cases even more serious than my own.

Closer to home, my life would be the poorer without the support of my wife, Nancey, my family and friends. I am even grateful to those who, from time to time, have made my life difficult, for they too have helped me to discover new ways of resolving my problems. Nor would I pretend that I have been the easiest person to live with, as many who read this book will testify. Frustrations, annoyances and irritations abound in the life of every blind person, and are often magnified beyond normality. As those who are without sight know only too well, being blind is not easy; but it need not be, I am glad to say, gloomy or depressing.

Even without sight, and with a 'hole in the head', life had to go on. Thankfully, life has gone on for me. 'Through the hole in my head' first came the offending bullet, then a gory mess of blood, pus and fragments of bone. After this life-shattering experience the remaking of my life began. From that point there had to be a new beginning. Once I regained consciousness, new perspectives on life and its prospects had to be formulated. New skills had to be learned, and new methods of coping had to be adopted. This was essential if life was going to hold any worthwhile future for me.

To claim that I have been more successful without sight than I might have been had I returned from the war with all my faculties may be an exaggeration. Who can tell what might have happened, and what direction my life might have taken?

My story is not dissimilar from many others brought about by the war, but setting it down in later life gives me the opportunity to pay tribute to those who have had a hand in my recovery, and who have enabled me to live life to the full, in spite of adverse circumstances. Without this multitude of helpers there would be no story to tell. It may also demonstrate that it is possible for a human being to survive a devastating head injury and still live a useful life. In spite of what some people claim, as far as I am concerned, mine is an ordinary story; all I have done is to have plodded on putting one foot in front of the other, and leaving the rest to prayer and to God.

1

Like nomads, we in the 2nd Battalion of the Border Regiment had been constantly on the move since leaving the Imphal area of Burma in October, pitching our makeshift squats every few days, clustered in a defensive formation around Company HQ. At each temporary stop slit-trenches were dug immediately, close to where we were to sleep. Look-out posts and patrols were also organised urgently. Every night, 'two hours on and four hours off' stints of guard duty had been the norm for each platoon since we entered the operational zone. On Christmas Day D Company, which I was in, snaked its way along the jungle tracks between the Chindwin and the Irrawaddy rivers. Two scouts led the way, armed with sten guns. The previous night, Christmas Eve, we had made camp at the entrance to the track, close to where two Japanese bodies had been buried with their skulls protruding out of the earth. The nights were awesomely silent, apart from the occasional barking of dogs in nearby villages, a warning sign to us that the Japs were stealthily on the move.

On Christmas Day itself, we were on our way at 2am for another gruelling 15-mile march through slippery silver sand, and before the day was finished I was called on to lead a forward patrol across a shallow river and through a perilously dangerous swamp, which almost cost us our lives. For weeks now we had hardly been out of our 'jungle greens', and we had become accustomed to sleeping rough. Water was at a premium. If we were lucky we did get a daily ration of heavily chlorinated water from the overworked battalion water truck, but we always took full advantage of every source of water to refill our water-bottles, wash our bodies and, if possible, our clothes. Water taken from brackish ponds, which was then heavily chlorinated, was often the only water available.

We were now just outside Satpangan, a small village on the banks of the River Irrawaddy. Mandalay was on the opposite bank, over 40 miles distant. Shortly after breakfast the Company was mustered by platoons, and orders were given for an immediate reconnaissance patrol. There were still pockets of dogged resistance from the Japanese rearguard. In the scrambled preparations there was little time to think about anything except the task now facing us. Our instructions were to reconnoitre the village close by. The bombers had been overhead, in the direction of Mandalay, and in the distance we could hear the thud of exploding bombs and the answering guns of the Japs as the action moved forward, but things seemed quiet enough where we were on the west bank of the river.

We moved in single file along the edges of the paddy-fields and got our first glimpse of the Irrawaddy just a few hundred yards ahead. As we came to the village we moved among the primitive houses raised above the ground on strong wooden stilts. Their terrified occupants abandoned them, visibly shaking with fear. It was hard to think, as we left our temporary camp that morning, that some of us might not return and that others would be carried from the battlefield by battalion stretcher-bearers. Our next objective was to make an advance towards a suspect emplacement a short distance from the village. We took up our position in the dried-up river bed under the command of Lieutenant Joe Bates, the Platoon Commander, and awaited his next order.

Tension mounted, and hearts began to beat faster. We had little to say to each other as we waited for the order to move, and that only in whispers. We were arranged by sections along the bank, which was just high enough to conceal us if we kept low. Lieutenant Bates gave the order to move, and I followed this with my own instructions, 'Come on, lads, let's go.' We sprang to the top of the bank still holding our rifles in readiness. No sooner had our heads risen above the top of the ditch than bullets from the concealed Jap marksmen began to come thick and fast. I shouted to the men, 'Get down. The bullets are coming pretty quick. I've got one through my hat.' Those were the last words I might ever have spoken. A bullet had, indeed, gone through my hat, but it had also gone right through my head just above my ears.

The men who were with me concluded that with such a severe wound, and with blood streaming from both sides of my head, I could not possibly survive. As a member of the platoon put it, 'Corporal Taylor's had it. We'll have to leave him.' In the meantime there was no let-up for them, as the fighting went on unabated until they were forced to withdraw, leaving me where I had fallen.

From then onwards, until I regained consciousness in a base hospital in Comilla two months later, I was oblivious of all sensation apart from one brief moment of semi-consciousness when I was aware of drinking my own urine while I was grovelling on the ground. I was in no-man's land, between my own Company and the enemy. I was not aware that the Japs had overrun our position, or that they had stripped me of my possessions, leaving me naked, until I was told of the sorry state in which I was found five days later – emaciated, and with my mouth covered in sores. How and why I survived, in defiance of all the laws of nature and of science, is an unsolved mystery. The nature of my wound, together with exposure and the lack of medical attention should have been enough to kill me. The Japs must have considered me dead, otherwise they would surely have put a bayonet through me to finish me off.

Arrangements for burials were already made when I was found. The battalion had by then driven the Japs across the river, and was under some pressure to keep up with them, before the burials were properly completed. According to my information, a senior Roman Catholic Chaplain from Brigade HQ requested that the dead should be decently buried before the move forward. It was when this was taking place that I was discovered and moved by flying jeep to the field hospital at Shwebo, where neuro-surgery took place under hypnosis.

Place, date, day and time of day did not begin to register again until I was almost out of my comatose state at the end of March. My return to consciousness and the partial recovery of sensation was slow, intermittent and excruciatingly painful. Only gradually did I begin to grasp where I was, and how I came to be there. When I eventually discovered that I was in the 92 Indian/British General Hospital my present life began to connect with previous events. I had been in one of the base hospitals in Comilla previously, when I had gone down with malaria. Since then I had travelled hundreds of miles by various modes of transport, and in all sorts of conditions, but the memory of leading my section forward and being shot came only by degrees.

As I tentatively awoke from my long sleep it was the crucifying headache which affected me most, as I cried out, 'My head; oh, my head!' There were similar incessant cries from those around me. I was too insensible at first to ask anyone why it was always dark. Sometimes I would feel the draping of the mosquito-net on my bed, but at other times it was not there. It was then that it began to dawn on me that I was not able to see anything. When I called out for attention, I heard voices at my side, but I did not see anyone. In my confusion I thought that it must still be night-time.

Once I was able to speak, doctors were frequently at my bedside. They put me through simple psychological tests, asking me questions I could not answer, and trying to learn from me what had happened when I was wounded, until I drifted off to sleep exhausted with the mental exertion. It was at this time that I had the first of a series of lumbar punctures – not a very pleasant experience. Nursing sisters dressed my wounds each morning, removing the thick layer of bandages which covered my head like a protective turban. From them, bit by bit, I learned about my condition, but I still thought then that my blindness would only be temporary, and that when my wounds had healed I would be returning to the front. I had to be convinced that this was improbable; I was on my way home, and my active service career was at an end.

During the mild spring sunshine, I was wheeled on to the veranda with some of my ward-mates, and learned from them something of their own battle experiences. Whilst I was still learning to walk again, word got around that some of us were being taken by air to Secunderabad, in South India for further treatment. We were to travel by air-ambulance. The final word to me from the ward sister was, 'Taylor, you are thin!' I had not been aware of my loss of weight, but I realise now that I must have looked very emaciated as I left the hospital.

During the flight more tiny fragments came to light about my recovery. One of the nurses quietly told me that she had been on duty when I showed the first signs of consciousness. The only other thing I remember about her was that she came from Sheffield. She is an important link in my story, and just one of my many unnamed benefactors. I had no further contact with her once we had been discharged from the plane, but without the involvement of such people there would be no story to tell.

A part of the story which no one could explain took place back in England on the day of the battle. My girlfriend's mother had a strange premonition that I was in trouble of some kind. The feeling was so strong that she woke her husband: 'Eric! I'm sure something has happened to Tom. We'll have to pray for him.' And being spiritually sensitive people with a firm Christian faith, this is what she and her husband did, in the middle of the night. It may be coincidental that she was moved to act in this way and at that particular time, but might not the question be asked, 'Was someone or something at work on my behalf?' Whilst all this was going on, word that I had been killed in action had reached my previous unit, the 7th King's Own Royal Regiment, then in Lahore, North India. My former colleagues of the battalion held a Memorial Service in my honour. They, in turn, passed on the rumour to their contacts in Workington, Cumberland, which eventually reached my girlfriend Nancey, who was devastated by the news. My own parents, however, only received confirmation of my situation when I had regained consciousness, and had begun to recover.

The battle of Satpangan went on for five days, and the battalion sustained a large number of dead and wounded casualties. More than 30 officers and men were killed and many more were wounded, some close to where I lay, and others at the other side of the Irrawaddy, once the river had been crossed. The names of those who lost their lives are recorded in the Roll of Honour in the Regimental Chapel in Carlisle Cathedral.

2

The transfer of our small group from Comilla to Trimulgerry in Secunderabad took place just before my 23rd birthday. Not yet able to walk unaided, I was being carried into an upstairs ward when one of the male orderlies remarked, 'Wouldn't it have been better if you had died?' I do not know how he was expecting me to reply, but to him I must have looked like a 'no hoper'. Thankfully for me, there were others who took a different attitude, who saw things differently and encouraged me in spite of my unpromising condition. Like those who had looked after me since I had been picked up, they were not going to let me slip away so easily. For that one man who saw me as a hopeless case, there were scores of others who did everything they could to save my life, even though they could never have anticipated the end result.

The doctors and surgeons wasted no time, and before I knew it there was a repetition of the clinical and psychological tests which I had undergone previously in Comilla, plus a few more. In addition, they took frequent X-rays of my skull from every angle, and electrodes were placed on my head to measure the activity of my brain, prior to further surgery. During the series of tests I realised for the first time that I now had no sense of smell or taste. In my weakened condition I did not appreciate the importance of these senses, nor had I made the connection between their loss and my head injury. It was only later that their full significance dawned on me.

But I do not recall being in any way anxious or afraid when I was being wheeled into the operating theatre for further surgery. I just took it all as part of the recovery process. The subsequent headache and sickness were more worrying, lest I burst open the stitches when vomiting.

Once I got on my feet after the final operation, step by step I began to find my way around the ward, counting the beds as I went along and acknowledging the voices which I slowly learned to recognise. Soon I was making my own way to the bathroom and toilets like the other men, first groping my way from bed to bed, colliding with people and obstacles until I picked up the echoing sound of men noisily chatting as they washed and shaved. It was a great achievement when I was able to shave myself once again. For the past weeks my daily shave had been carried out by the hospital barber, an Indian, with a cut throat razor, but in spite of his best efforts I was not completely satisfied that he had done a proper job. This was not the first time I had shaved without seeing my face; it was common practice to shave without the use of a mirror whilst we were on the move in Burma, so now when a mirror was no longer any use to me I got a lot of pleasure from knowing that my chin was as smooth as it had been for a Company Inspection.

When it was suggested that I should start doing some physical exercises I thought it was a joke. However, Miss Margerson, the physiotherapist in charge, assured me that the exercises would be beneficial. I progressed in stages from simple stretching movements of my arms and legs on my bed to more strenuous exercises on the floor. These performances seemed to give some encouragement to the medical and nursing staff, who were surprised by my rapidly increasing agility. One of the nursing sisters even persuaded me to try riding a bicycle, but this ended in failure because I now had no sense of balance.

It was during this period, less than three months after my bullet wound, that I made my first contact with St Dunstan's, but it was not until the following year that I entered the organisation fully, to begin my training. St Dunstan's was established during the first world war to meet the needs of the large number of individuals who had lost their eyesight as a result of their war service. It was founded by Sir Arthur Pearson in 1915, and since then has continued its work of training and welfare. Shortly after my arrival in Trimulgerry the ward sister brought a man to my bedside, who introduced himself as St Dunstan's representative in that part of India. My only knowledge of St Dunstan's up to that time came from an article in a weekly illustrated magazine which, strangely enough, I had been reading shortly before I lost my eyesight. My visitor put a Braille pocket watch in my hand. It was shaped like any other pocket watch, but its dial and fingers were covered in a hinged, steel casing instead of glass, with raised dots marking the figures and strong fingers capable of withstanding frequent handling. After he had showed me how to use it he said, 'This watch is on loan whilst you are here, but when you return to England, St Dunstan's will give you one for your personal use.' I was amazed by the small device in my hand. It was such a small thing, but to me it represented a quantum leap in independence. It was marvellous to know what time of day it was without troubling anyone. It was even more gratifying to be able to tell others the time when they asked.

In the quiet orderly routine of the ward it was possible to believe that the war had already ended, but this illusion was shattered when the wards began to fill up with more casualties and men released from Japanese prison camps, with their accounts of malnutrition and its associated diseases, and even more terrible stories of men being buried alive. The Fourteenth Army, under the leadership of General Slim, had now advanced as far as Rangoon, and with that major objective behind them came some respite for the front-line troops. Fortunately for me, the 2nd Borders spent their rest period in the Secunderabad area. I was completely taken by surprise one day, when several of my own section appeared at my bedside, bringing me up to date about the battalion with the grim news about all the dead and wounded since my own departure from the action.

Although I was still coming to terms with the adjustments I was having to make, I began to pick up the threads from where my life had changed on the edge of the village of Satpangan. The news bulletins on All India Radio informed us that the war in Europe was coming to an end, and although I was unable to feel any personal involvement in what was happening thousands of miles away, there was, nevertheless, a glimmer of hope that war throughout the world would soon be over.

When Victory in Europe came in May, the rejoicing on the ward was tremendous. A celebration dance was arranged in the hospital grounds for patients and staff. I was escorted there in my hospital-blues by one of the nursing sisters. In spite of the length of time since I had last taken the floor, and the fact that I could not now see in which direction I was going, I managed a few quicksteps and waltzes, and I did not lack dancing partners during the evening, which flattered my ego just a little. With this accomplishment, and the stimulating support of everyone, I was encouraged to attempt other more adventurous things.

If St Dunstan's was to be my finishing school, then the Indian Red Cross Society must be given the credit as my primary school for starting my return to life in the real world, especially the ladies who staffed the occupational therapy unit attached to the hospital. This was a multi-racial group of women: Indian, Anglo-Indian, Irish and British, who encouraged the patients in their first steps towards rehabilitation. For myself and some of the others on the

ward it really was like starting again in the infant class, as we learned how to make small woolly toys before advancing to more complicated handicrafts. The Red Cross lady, who went round the ward each morning with her trolley full of materials, thought us an unpromising bunch of clients, as most of us thought the work a bit too infantile for grown men. However, when it was realised that we could win the hearts of the nurses by making useful presents for them, we were much keener to have a go. When I left India the Red Cross ladies presented me with a leather wallet which they had made, bearing the embossed emblems of India: the lotus flower and an Indian dancing girl, together with my own scrawly signature, my first effort at writing my name without sight.

The hospital patients were invited to a variety of social functions. We were frequent visitors to the palace of the Nizam of Hyderabad state, as guests of His Exalted Highness. Celebrity artistes and well-known entertainers from ENSA also put on shows for us. Some of these events were embarrassing for me, when I found myself in the privileged position of occupying a centre seat of the front row, usually reserved for the higher ranks and their wives. It was even more embarrassing when I was asked to give the vote of thanks on behalf of the assembled company, my first faltering attempts at public speaking. I cannot pretend that I did not enjoy this preferential treatment, and there was no questioning the therapeutic value of the attention I was getting, but I realised that this kind of mollycoddling could not go on for ever. Sooner or later I had to face the harsher realities of living with my head injury and my blindness.

The surgeon confirmed that the damage to my sensory organs was irreversible and that my blindness would be permanent. I would be unlikely to resume a fully normal life as before. Everything was fine whilst I was in the care and security of the hospital environment, but a time would come when these props would no longer be there, and I would have to learn to cope with my responsibilities on my return to civilian life. I was not fully aware at the time what this would mean. From now on, I would have to get used to the idea of being more dependent on other people for many of my basic needs, which in turn would affect my self-respect and self-confidence.

At the beginning of July I was considered fit enough for repatriation. The powers-that-be decided that I should travel by train with an escort as far as Bombay, and continue by air to the UK. After a few more days I said my farewells to my well-wishers and set off on my way home.

When I had my eyesight, I found travelling by rail in India an interesting experience. Every trip was a study in human behaviour: observing the milling crowds in colourful, assorted garments scrambling for places on already overcrowded trains, and performing all manner of tasks at the railway stations, from cooking meals, to haircutting and shampooing. But as I travelled to Bombay now, in the exclusive first-class compartment provided for me and my RAF escort, I could still hear the noise of the jostling masses at each stop, but I was not now part of the swirling throng, nor could I appreciate the distinctive Indian aromas. The excitement on this occasion had nothing at all to do with the travelling multitudes, but with the millions of hungry ants inside the compartment, though they did not really bother us until we wanted to eat. We had been provided with sufficient food for the whole journey, but when we came to eat our bully beef sandwiches we discovered to our dismay that millions of tiny ants had got to them first. Unfortunately I had taken my first bite before they were spotted. My mouth was soon full of angry ants eating away at the inside of my mouth, leaving it swollen and tingling, much worse than any nettle-sting. For me it was a lesson well learned, and ever since I have been ultra-cautious about what goes into my mouth.

On our arrival in Bombay, members of the medical staff from the RAF hospital were there to meet us. I then became their responsibility for the next stage of my journey. Being moved from place to place with an escort was something else I had to get used to. I was no longer a free agent able to move about as I pleased; at least until I had learned some mobility skills.

I had always been fascinated by India, its customs and cultures, since the moment I arrived there several years before on the troop ship, *Dempo*. I was now leaving it with many vivid and varied memories. Quite literally, I had come of age whilst I was there, and had matured as a person through a wealth of enriching experiences. My perception of this brief final period in Bombay contrasted sharply with my first impressions. Then I saw everything with my own eyes. It struck me immediately as a land of extremes: the beautiful, ornamental 'Gateway to India' symbolising the opulence and grandeur on the one hand; and the barely clothed 'coolies' and the crippled, misshapen bodies of the street beggars, revealing a great depth of poverty on the other.

Travelling back to the UK by air was both a privilege and an adventure. Apart from my RAF companion, my fellow travellers remained anonymous; I suspected that most of them were high ranking military officers or government officials. Ordinary people like myself did not travel by air in those days. The sea voyage to India, including a few weeks' break in South Africa, took over three months; the return home was completed in three days and in just over 30 hours' flying time. The need for frequent refuelling meant that the journey was completed in several stages, with brief stops at places which I remembered from my geography lessons at school: Cairo, Malta, Bahrain, Baghdad, El Alem and Marseilles. Visiting these places stretched my imagination as I tried to picture what they were like. Crossing the English Channel on our approach to Poole in Dorset, then one of the main airports for passenger traffic, triggered off a typical British conversation about the weather. The grey clouds and the misty drizzle through which we were passing, and the lush greenness of the meadows below us were in complete contrast to the desert wastelands over which we had passed. The gentle rain on my face as I came down the steps of the plane was a welcome sign that I was really back home in England. It was early July, but it seemed so cold in comparison to the sweltering heat of India which I had left only three days before, and I wondered how long it would take me to get re-acclimatised to the cooler, damper atmosphere.

No sooner had the plane come to a standstill on the runway than I was separated from my RAF helper; I hardly time to say goodbye to him and thank him for his companionship. Soon I was being whisked through customs after which I was handed over to the driver of a waiting army ambulance, along with my kitbag and medical notes. Within a matter of minutes I was travelling through the lanes of Dorset to a large country house in Shaftesbury, temporarily requisitioned as a war-time hospital. The nurses there were very good in helping me to cope with my new surroundings, but I found the routine of the wards a bit more restrictive than I had been used to in India, and I chafed a little at the extra discipline. This more regimented life was something I would have to accept for the few remaining weeks of my army service.

I was transferred to St Hugh's Military Hospital in Oxford 48 hours later. Travelling along the English country roads again on that bright summer morning it was almost as if everything in my life was returning to normal. It was market day in the small town where we stopped for coffee. As I took in this typical piece of English life, listening to the bustle and chatter of housewives busy about their shopping, there was no mistaking that I was truly back in England.

3

My introduction to St Hugh's was inauspicious. I was in trouble even before I reached the reception desk, and came dangerously close to losing my exemplary army record. As I entered the building for the first time, escorted by the young lady who had brought me from Shaftesbury, someone grabbed hold of the lapels of my battle dress, and upbraided me for insubordination and for being improperly dressed. Not being able to see who was shouting at me, I assumed that it was the duty officer. If so, my failure to salute him would amount to insubordination, and the outfit I was wearing, which had been supplied by the hospital stores in India, consisting of an Australian bush hat, a new khaki battledress - showing no badge of rank and not properly fastened - and a pair of officer's brown boots, made me improperly dressed. I had become so accustomed by this time to everyone treating me with less formality that the abrupt change of attitude momentarily stunned me. I thought that he was going to have me put on a charge for my indiscipline, but for the timely and coincidental appearance of Major McGregor, the doctor who had performed the operation on my head when I was brought in from the battlefield in Burma. It was fortunate that he was there at that moment to intervene on my behalf and to give a brief account of my injuries and the cause of my blindness. From then on things went more smoothly for me, though my life at St Hugh's was more regimented than I had previously experienced.

I was assigned to one of the medical wards. As I was being taken to my bed I was intrigued by all the convolutions, set at peculiar angles, in the passageways leading to that part of the hospital. The wards were temporary brick-built annexes of the main building. These were arranged between the trees in the extensive college grounds. Apparently, the trees were protected by preservation orders, hence the contorted system of corridors circumventing the wards.

As a blind person, going into the ward for the first time was an intimidating experience. Under normal circumstances it would not have bothered me. Before I lost my eyesight I had no difficulty in introducing myself to people, as well as noting automatically the layout of a room, its furniture and the situation of doors and windows. However, circumstances were not normal, so none of this applied – I could no longer see. Although I could differentiate between darkness and light, I was unable to recognise anything visually, either by shape, size or position. At times, because of the unusual nature of my blindness – damage to the occupational cortex – my eyes appeared deceptively normal, which had awkward and sometimes embarrassing consequences.

For the first few days in the ward I was regarded as something of an oddity and most of the men kept their distance from me. It was as if they did not quite know how to approach a blind person. In this hospital ward I came face to face with a group of complete strangers in a new and bewildering location. This was an elementary and essential lesson in the recovery of my independence. From now on, I would need to earn my 'place in the sun'. It was obvious that I was not likely to be automatically accepted as a group member. Hitherto, I had enjoyed all the extra attention I was getting but now it was beginning to dawn on me that things were not going to revolve around me as they had done in my cosy, comfortable cocoon. It was time to face the fact that I could not assume that everyone I met would treat me with kid gloves. At this stage it would have been easy to lapse into self-pity.

Apart from Dennis in the next bed but one, most of the other patients were not war casualties. Dennis was the first person in the ward to make himself known to me. He was a young Welsh lad, badly crippled from a spinal wound which had also affected his speech. We got on well together. I met him again many years later when he became a resident at St Dunstan's when his eyesight had deteriorated. Cecil, another man on the ward with whom I became friendly, was a Cumbrian like my girlfriend,

Nancey. Unfortunately he did not survive an operation to remove a cerebral tumour, and died in the hospital.

There was nothing further from my mind, as I lay on my bed only two or three days later, than to hear the voices of my parents, and I dismissed it as an illusion when I thought I recognised their unmistakable Lancashire accents as they approached the ward. But sure enough it was them, and within seconds there was an emotional reunion. It had been three years since I had last seen them, but I had no difficulty in identifying their voices, and could still picture their physical features in my mind as they came closer to my bed. My first thought was, 'However have they managed to get here so quickly?' when I had only let them know where I was the previous day. Apparently, because I was still in the seriously ill category, the hospital authorities had sent them a telegram as soon as I had arrived in England and had made all the arrangements for their visit, including a travel warrant and accommodation.

The 'seriously ill' message had brought my parents quickly to Oxford and they were pleasantly surprised to find me out of bed, dressed and moving hesitantly about the ward. Although my hair was closely cropped from my last operation and my head still needed some protection, my general condition was stable and I felt fairly well in myself, considering what I had experienced during the past few months.

It was natural, at first, for them to show concern for me, but even at this stage there was a danger that they might become overprotective. The last thing I wanted was for them to become sentimental and maudlin towards me. I felt that they were keenly eyeing my every movement, ready to shout a warning whenever I approached an obstacle. I could easily become less independent if I was not permitted to do things for myself, to make my own mistakes, have my knocks and bruises, and even my calamities. In time I would have to show them that learning how to negotiate my way around furniture and to trace my way unaided was part of my re-education. It was hard for them, therefore, when they wanted to do even the smallest task for me, and I was trying to do as much for myself as possible.

Following the happy reunion with my parents, I was hoping for a similar joyful event when Nancey and her mother arrived at St Hugh's not many days after my parents returned home. Although I was more prepared for their visit I had some twinges of anxiety about this first meeting with Nancey since I had lost my sight, wondering how it would be when we came face to face. Nancey and I had been corresponding regularly since I had been stationed in Workington, but as we had hardly known each other at that point, our relationship had not progressed much further than that of mutual attraction. Since I had been wounded, this correspondence could only be continued with the help of a third-party. This inhibited us both from expressing our thoughts as openly and freely as we might have done otherwise, so I was careful about who I asked to write and to read my letters for me, and I was grateful to those who helped me. We had not made any plans for the future prior to this visit, just an understanding that the relationship might continue. Nancey, too, may have had her apprehensions, and I ought not to take for granted that her feelings were still the same towards me now that I was without eyesight and with an uncertain future. If the relationship were to develop, she would have to take a lot on trust.

When she arrived, for a brief period the days were brilliantly sunny and cloudless – really and metaphorically – and it was much easier to put aside thoughts of the future, to enjoy the present and get to know one another a little more. The days spent by the river in Oxford were idyllic in every sense, and before Nancey and her mother left for Cumberland we had agreed to announce our engagement in the near future, possibly when I arrived in Workington on hospital leave.

I had had no normal leave since leaving the UK three years before, but now there was a possibility of going home for a few weeks, provided that this met with the approval of the medical authorities. There were still some investigations to be completed, including the dreaded lumbar puncture. Once these were out of the way the doctors in charge of the ward raised no objections to me going home for a few weeks. Before I started my leave early in August I was told that as St Hugh's was being restored as a University college, the head injuries unit was being transferred to the Churchill Hospital at Headington during my absence, and that I would be going direct to the Churchill at the end of my leave. The hospital authorities did their best to ensure that my journey home was as comfortable and easy as possible. I had the exclusive use of a third-class compartment on the train, and the elderly Red Cross lady who escorted me was the ideal person for the job. She protected the compartment whenever intruders threatened to invade my privacy, and got me all the help I needed from the railway staff.

There had been plenty of time over the past months to imagine what my homecoming would be like. Before I was injured there had always been that thrill of anticipation of arriving on leave: leaping from the bus just a few yards from home with my kitbag on my shoulder, and seeing the astonished faces of the family as I burst through the living-room door. How different it would be this time, arriving by taxi, and being guided by a uniformed Red Cross lady. I was still as excited about going home as I had been formerly, but now there were the reactions of my brothers and sister and the rest of my family to cope with. I would be unable to see the smiles of welcome on their faces. Worse, would I be able to recognise them easily by their voices?

It was late in the afternoon when my escort delivered me to my home in Bury. It had been a long day, and I was hoping that there would not be too much fuss, but it was not to be. When I arrived, the living-room was already full of people: my parents and grandmother, my brothers and sister, uncles, aunts and cousins, plus friends and neighbours. It was difficult at first sorting out who was who in the babble of conversation and plethora of voices, but I soon began to recognise most of them. Two voices, however, were strange to me. My younger brother, Jack, was still a schoolboy with an unbroken treble voice when I went overseas; now he was a tall, young working man with a baritone voice. My sister-in-law Kathleen's voice was also completely new to me; she and my brother Fred had been married during my period of oblivion in February and this was the first time I had met her. My return home had also aroused some local interest. News had got around that Tom Taylor, who had been blinded in Burma, was coming home, and people were curious about me.

Some of the pleasures I had been most looking forward to were sleeping in a civilian bed for the first time for several years, escaping from routine for a few weeks and enjoying an occasional lie-in. The thought of this luxury was enhanced when I found that a new bed had been bought to mark my homecoming.

None of my family had any previous experience of blindness, and my arrival back home made a difference to their pattern of life. I could not expect them to change things round completely to suit me, nor did I want to be treated like a piece of Dresden china; too delicate to touch, and too sensitive to criticism. But everyone tried to be as helpful as they could and in return I had to accept certain restrictions and acknowledge my limitations. The family had to adjust to having me around the house most of the time, with the extra demands which my blindness placed upon them. Being confined to my chair in the corner made me feel even less in control of things than I had done for some time. I could not imagine myself lounging about in an armchair for very long, confined to that small living-room. My restlessness and impatience would begin to get the better of me if there was nothing for me to do except to eat, sleep, make my little woolly toys and listen to the radio. It was unthinkable that I should even consider venturing out of doors alone. I could not read a book or a newspaper, or share in any activity with a visual content.

It was frustrating too not being able to write freely to Nancey. The only means I had of keeping in touch with her directly was by telephone, and even this had many drawbacks. Neither of us had direct access to a telephone, and we had to depend on the goodwill of relatives and friends until I had overcome the problem of getting to the telephone box unaided, and I had mastered the simple technique of manipulating the coins and buttons. This was not an ideal arrangement, as it was quite impossible to hold a private conversation.

My next aim was to get to Workington, as Nancey and I had already agreed that part of my leave should be spent with her and her family. I was not yet capable of making the journey unattended, so I had to explore other means of getting there. Going by train with a member of the family seemed the simplest, but for some reason this was impracticable at the time. Another option was to be taken by car. All my relatives had already expressed their eagerness to help me, and this was one way they could give me some practical assistance, the only snag being the current shortage of petrol. Petrol was still strictly rationed by coupon and few people had a sufficient fuel allowance to make a double round trip of over 400 miles. The problem was solved when we discovered that if I possessed a car, I could claim a concessionary petrol allowance which was available to members of the services when on leave. My Uncle Tom kindly transferred the registration of his black and green Morris 10 to my name for the duration of my leave. Of course, my uncle had to drive the car.

Early on a Sunday morning just two weeks into my leave, we set out for Cumberland, my Uncle Tom and Auntie Doris, my father and me. It was a mild and pleasant morning, and ideal for motoring through the Lake District. The roads were almost as quiet as the mountains and valleys. We passed through towns and villages which until now had been only names on a map: Windermere, Ambleside, Grasmere. Only when we got through Keswick could I begin to relate to the landscape. Wythop and Sale Fell and had been army training areas and I could accurately visualise them, because it was on those rocky hillsides where we had our final spell of training before going overseas. There was something familiar about the twists and bends in the road as we came into the town. I still had a map of Workington imprinted in my memory and was able to act as navigator for the last few hundred yards of the journey.

As a serving soldier I did not think I would ever return to Workington, but here I was, to establish a permanent link by persuading one of its daughters to become my wife. It was an important time in world history and it was also a very significant one for Nancey and me. My visit coincided with the surrender of the Japanese forces, which brought the second world war to an official end. Nancey and I began to plan more seriously for our wedding day, which was to be 14th September the following year. During the visit I became better acquainted with my future in-laws, and wider circle of relations. I had met several of them during my service days when I was fit and active, and things were normal. Now they were seeing me under different circumstances - much less active and more physically dependent. Nancey had several aunts, uncles and cousins so it was difficult for me at first to put names to voices. Once the news had got around that Nancey and I were getting married we had many goodwill messages, although one or two people might have had some reservations about Nancey's decision to marry a blind man with a head wound and with no guaranteed future.

After we had visited Nancey's relations we were free to revisit some of the places associated with my army days. Waves of nostalgia hit me as I walked through the gates of Workington Hall, through which I had marched on that cold December night en route for Avonmouth, South Africa and India. The gravel driveway up to the Hall still crunched under my feet, and my voice in the quadrangle still echoed around as it had done when I had issued drill commands a few years earlier. I had to remind myself that I was still in the army, though no longer able to perform the duties of a soldier.

All too soon my weeks of freedom came to an end. The final day in Workington was a double celebration: Nancey's mother's birthday, and the announcement of our engagement. My mother was there – along with my sister Peggy – and was happy because she too had now met Nancey.

The Churchill Hospital in Headington, to which I returned after my leave, was a modern building, formerly used by the Americans. My bed was next to the Sister's office, and my companion on the other side was a newly admitted patient, Tom Mitchell, a jokey young Irish lad from Lurgan. He became my unpaid assistant for the remainder of my stay. Most of his time was spent in occupational therapy when he was not looking after me. When I first met him, he was putting the finishing touches to a little ornament, a fish made out of perspex. I assumed it was for someone special, judging by the care and attention he was giving to it. He must have noticed my interest in what he was doing, but said nothing. Several weeks later, after I had been transferred to Stoke Mandeville Hospital, I discovered this beautiful fish, carefully wrapped and without a label, at the bottom of my kitbag. Tom had slipped it in with my clothes when he helped me to pack before leaving the Churchill Hospital; such was his generosity. Regrettably, I never had the chance to thank him.

The Free Church Chaplain to the hospital, Norman Priestley, a Methodist minister, visited me shortly after my return, and immediately he spoke I recognised a fellow Lancastrian. He seemed very interested in my story and did not see why I might not, at some time in the future, take up work in the Church, possibly as a youth leader. He offered to make further enquiries on my behalf, but the doctors and medical staff were dismissive of the idea, and I was too, not only because of my blindness, but because of my lack of educational attainments. I met Mr Priestley again many years later, when I had become a local preacher in the Methodist Church under his superintendency.

Nothing more could be done for me by way of medical treatment. I was told that I was being transferred to the Ministry of Pensions hospital at Stoke Mandeville where I would be discharged from the services, on medical grounds.

4

I had mixed feelings as I was being transferred to the Stoke Mandeville Hospital in Aylesbury. During the 25-mile journey there was time to recollect my fortunes and misfortunes of the past nine months, and to consider the next stage in my progress towards my return to civilian life. Until I was wounded I was physically fit, and in the top medical category, 'A1'. As we passed through the gates of the hospital and up the long drive, the thought passed through my mind, 'Am I soon to become another of society's rejects and from now on be of little further use to anyone?' I had been lucky to survive a severe head injury, but what did the future hold in store? According to the general medical opinion from St Hugh's, my long-term prospects were not very great, in spite of my steady progress. They felt that the best I could hope for was to spend my time in simple handicraft work, and possibly to learn Braille and typewriting.

Several times during recent weeks self-pity had threatened to make me feel sorry for myself; it was becoming too easy to become preoccupied with my own small world. I had already accepted that I could no longer take refuge in the cushioned nursing environment and that sooner or later I would have to take my part in the world as a responsible human being. Stoke Mandeville was my point of transition from my secure life in the army to a more precarious life in Civvy Street.

The war had been over now for several months, and like everyone else I was thankful that it was so. Now a wave of anticlimax swept through everything, and people began to forget the privations and the sacrifices of the past six years. The indifference among those who had been unaffected by loss or injury quickly showed itself. Those who had suffered the death of a loved one were left to their solitary mourning. The war casualties had to pick up the broken pieces of their lives and get on with what was left with the help of their families and various organisations. Those of us who returned home with war wounds also wanted to forget what had happened but that was impossible. However one attempted to minimise its effect or compensate for the loss, what had happened was a physical fact which had to be endured for the rest of one's life.

War disabilities also affected social relationships. I just wanted to be accepted by others as a fellow human, still capable of making a valid contribution to society. I knew of many disabled war veterans who had overcome their physical handicaps and had proved themselves to be valued and respected citizens. I had no idea what the future held for me by way of employment or occupation. I had known men of my own generation who had been badly injured who had been able to go back to their old jobs, with help. In my case this seemed most unlikely. I had not seriously thought about returning to my job as a printer, believing that my disability was enough to exclude me from that. One thing that I had considered was poultry farming, though I did not know if it would be possible for me even to be trained.

Up to this point I had been the only blind patient in each of the hospitals I had been in, and because of this I had attracted a lot of sympathy. From now on I had to realise that I was just one of many, and that I was literally surrounded by people without sight. The causes of my own blindness may have been unique, but the awful truth soon dawned on me that the cruelties of war had caused even greater injuries to many more people than myself. Invariably, those who are blinded in battle conditions have multiple disabilities to cope with. It was not just a matter of loss of sight, but injury to or loss of other faculties. In my case it was the holes in my head and the loss of my senses of taste and smell which complicated the problem. With others it was the loss of hearing or the amputation of a limb. My own afflictions were not immediately obvious, whilst others who had caught the full blast of an exploding bomb or land mine were visibly scarred for life. And each one of us was affected to some degree by nervous trauma. If I had felt any lingering self-pity or egotism, it faded away after I had been introduced to my new ward-mates in the St Dunstan's wing at Stoke Mandeville. There were probably then 30 or 40 war-blinded patients in these two special wards. All of them, like myself, were awaiting their final medical board, before training for their vocational occupations at St Dunstan's, which was then based at Church Stretton in Shropshire.

I was not altogether prepared for what I found on going into the St Dunstan's wing. I had not previously been in contact with many blind people. During my time in India I had seen many blind beggars, and I had vague recollections from my childhood of 'blind Johnnie' tapping his way along our street delivering his morning newspapers; he was just one of the 'odd' characters of my childhood. Then there was Blind Ernest, who sold newspapers in the centre of the town. Everyone knew him. He called out the latest news on the street corner, with all his papers piled up on the window-ledge of a public house. He was always there, whatever the weather. I often wondered how he coped amid all the noise and confusion going on around him. His eyes were always open wide – white eyeballs streaked with red blood-vessels. My attitude towards blind people in those days was very similar to what I suppose the general public's attitude is towards blind people today. I had no real feeling for them until I became one of their number. My time at Stoke Mandeville changed all this, and I was forced to alter my attitude to other blind people both as individuals and in communities.

The atmosphere of the ward was completely different from what I had expected. Instead of a cloistered quiet hospital, there was raucous healthy laughter and loud verbal banter and chit-chat going on everywhere. 'These men may have lost their sight,' I thought, 'but they haven't lost their voices, and certainly not their sense of humour!' It was very much the same as it had been in many an army barrack room where it only needed the right mix of people to make the place come alive, and this place was indeed very much alive. It was hard to believe that these men who had lost their sight had, until recently been on active service in Europe, the Middle East or the Far East – on land, on sea, or in the air. Here was a microcosm of the British fighting forces, representatives of the war-scarred British nation. There were Lancastrians, Yorkshiremen, Cockneys and men from many other parts of this country and other British Commonwealth countries.

This my introduction to a completely new experience, and also my first meeting with the remarkable family of St Dunstan's. Many of the men to whom I was introduced that day have become friends and colleagues as the years have passed. Just as we differed in the nature of our injuries and our social and geographical backgrounds, so we differed in our personalities and temperaments, as widely as the members of any family.

St Dunstan's was so efficient that I wasn't given much time to mope or brood. I hardly had time to unpack before I was being whisked away for my first Braille lesson. Just as I was considering taking an afternoon nap after my journey from Oxford, a voice at my side said, in an unmistakable Yorkshire accent, 'I believe you are Tom Taylor! I am George Killingbeck, the Braille teacher, and I would like to introduce you to Braille.' I had no time to object, and before I knew what was happening I was being led away by this comparative stranger to a table in the centre of the room and seated on a hard wooden seat. George Killingbeck sat down beside me, took my right hand, palm downwards, opened up my fingers and placed them on a sheet of stiff paper which seemed to be covered with a mass of haphazardly arranged breadcrumbs. This was my introduction to the Braille system, and it meant absolutely nothing to me. It was just an incomprehensible mass of dots. My inclination was to get up from the table and quit Braille for ever, but I am thankful that I persevered. At first I thought that I would never be able to master it, but George Killingbeck was persuasive and infinitely patient with beginners. By the end of that first half-hour session I felt that my head was swimming in a sea of little pimples. It was to George's credit, however, that I could now identify the first three letters of the Braille alphabet by touch.

At the age of 23 I was back at the A-B-C stage of learning to read and write. The Braille system is based on a series of six raised dots arranged in two vertical columns of three, similar to the blank/six of a domino. For teaching purposes, these are numbered one to three in the left column and four to six in the right column. The first 10 letters of the alphabet are formed from dots one, two, four and five - thus, dot one equals A; dots one and two equals B; dots one and three equals C, and so on.

With practice and experience I began to recognise the patterns that formed the letters, and when words and sentences began to make sense I felt that I was really getting somewhere. It was only later that I began fully to appreciate the value of this tactile code, which was devised by the young blind Frenchman, Louis Braille, more than a hundred years before I was born. Louis Braille had lost his sight as a boy, whilst playing with a sharp instrument in his father's leather shop. As sad as this misfortune was, his ingenuity has been of great benefit to countless millions of blind people.

Before I left Stoke Mandeville, George gave me an elementary reading book, *The Divers*, in Grade 1 (uncontracted) Braille, to keep me going until I started my training course at Church Stretton. Fully contracted Braille is a much more complex system than Grade 1, and it was another six months, when I was in full training, before I had learned the full range of Braille symbols and their values. It was much longer before I dared consider myself a proficient Braillist. Nevertheless, I could see from the beginning that mastery of the Braille code was fundamental to my search for independence.

I have more than one reason to be grateful to George. Apart from the fact that he opened up new avenues for me through Braille, he was the first blind person I had met who showed me that it was possible to live a 'normal' social life. I did not even realise that he was blind until several days after our initial meeting. He seemed to move easily from place to place, and he spoke as though he was seeing everything around him with uncanny normality. More than this, all the time he was teaching me I did not realise that he had only one hand, and that even this had several fingers missing. George had lost his sight and an arm in the First World War, but this had not prevented him from living a full and useful life, mostly in the service of other people.

At Stoke Mandeville typewriting was taught alongside Braille. I soon came face to face with the typewriter keyboard, and was taught the basics of touch-typing. I was excited at the thought that I would soon be able to write my own letters, so it was disappointing that in my first lesson I did nothing more than learn how to insert the paper in the machine, adjust it, and set the margins and tabulations. I had hoped to learn the whole keyboard in one go, so that I could impress the people back home with my progress. I thought that all that was necessary was to sit behind the typewriter and that it would all come to me like magic, but I soon found out that it wasn't going to be as easy as that. Typing, like every other skill, required discipline and practice. My teacher, a softly-spoken Canadian woman, insisted on getting the essentials correct from the start.

There were always machines available for people who wanted to have a go on their own. As soon as I thought I was familiar enough with the keyboard, and regardless of typing errors, I sent my unchecked letters to Nancey and my family. I blush to remember some of the hilarious mistakes those first letters contained, but those at home realised that efforts were being made to give me some independence in writing, which had not been possible since my last letters from Burma at the beginning of the year.

Encouraged by the staff, and people like George Killingbeck, I decided to take the initiative and test my ability to function on my own. There was no objection when I applied for a 'weekend pass' to visit Nancey in

Workington. This would be my first unescorted railway journey since becoming blind – a distance of 300 miles with a change at Carlisle. I was a little worried about travelling alone, but if I could have some help changing trains and someone to meet me in Workington, there should not be any difficulty.

All the arrangements were made. A member of St Dunstan's staff was to help me get on the train at Aylesbury, friends of Nancey's family would help me transfer to the local train at Carlisle, and Nancey would be at the Workington end to meet me. But sadly, this journey never got beyond the planning stage. It was just after 10 o'clock on the Friday morning, two hours before I was due to start my journey. I was keyed up with excitement at the prospect of what was for me a daunting adventure: to travel unaccompanied on a journey of over 300 miles, without being able to see. Just two more hours and then I would be off. I was laughing and trying to make light of what lay ahead of me, when a voice at my side spoke to me. It was the voice of Lady Fraser, the wife of Sir Ian Fraser, the Chairman of St Dunstan's. She said, 'I think you had better sit down. I have some very sad news for you.' I sat on the edge of my bed, and she began to tell me quietly and sympathetically that my father had died earlier that morning.

She held my hand for a long time whilst I tried to take in what she was saying to me. I sat devastated, leaning forward with my head bent over in a stunned silence, unable to accept what I was hearing. I just could not believe it. Only a few weeks before my father and I had been discussing plans for my future once I was back home. Now all that we had talked about was meaningless. I remembered reading – when I had had my sight – a moving story about a young soldier returning from service in India, whose father had died only a few days before he arrived home, and who like myself was to be invalided from the army. I thought about the cruel irony of this story in the days that followed.

In the previous week I had written home to tell my parents about my trip to Cumberland, thinking that they would be pleased. Had I known that my father was dangerously ill I would have been hastening to Bury instead of Workington, but I was unaware of how serious things were. No doubt it was to spare me any anxiety that no one informed me of his condition but I would have found it easier to accept his death had I been able to see him during his last days.

The following days were lived in a fog of misery. My return home was hastily arranged and a Red Cross volunteer escorted me as far as Manchester. My sister, younger brother and cousin John met me at the station and we drove back home almost in silence; our mood and conversation matching the gloomy November night. The house, too, was cheerless, filled again with family, relatives and friends who had called to console my mother. Almost the same people were there as three months earlier when I arrived back from the Far East, but now everyone was talking in whispers, recalling personal anecdotes about Fred, as my father was always known.

I spent some moments alone at the bedside where my father lay, trying to convince myself that it was really him, as my fingers traced the cold contours of his face. I could not be mistaken now – this was my father – the firm chin and the aquiline nose, the high cheek-bones and forehead; his hair still parted at the side, tufted and wiry, just as I had always remembered it. It was here that I said my final goodbye, and all my vivid memories of him returned as I did so.

His family was working-class, and he never made claims to sainthood. I have a mental picture of him with floury hands, in his spotlessly white apron working in the bake-house of my grandma's shop. For health reasons he had to quit this occupation, and during the Depression of the 1930s he was one of the millions of unemployed. He and my mother started a small hardware business to make provision for themselves and four growing children, until he found a job as a cotton operative in a local mill. I cannot remember a time when he did not have his garden plot, and his chicken-run with his dozen Rhode Island Reds; it was my job to feed them on my way to school.

I drifted along with the funeral arrangements and all the comings and goings, frustrated that I could not share in any of the practical arrangements. Was I now always going to be inadequate in coping with everyday business matters?

It was a raw, bright November morning when we buried him. He would have smiled at the long line of cars which joined the cortège to the cemetery, and the large number of friends who came to pay their last respects.

Shortly after the funeral I was back in Stoke Mandeville for my final medical board, a formality which was completed within minutes. I was discharged from the army on medical grounds and awarded a hundred per cent War Disability pension, with constant attendance allowance, the total amounting to £2 10s! The following day I was taken to Olympia in London, then being used as a demobilisation centre, and given a full civilian rig-out – socks, shoes, shirt, tie, suit, raincoat, and trilby hat – which would transform me into a normal citizen once again. I was also given civilian ration books, clothing and sweet coupons, and other essential documents. Back at Stoke Mandeville I tried on my new clothes, and realised that very soon the army would have no further claims on me. The cease-fire had now been declared, but I still had a fight on my hands, and more subtle enemies to defeat: boredom and self-pity.

Three weeks before Christmas I finally arrived home. The streets were miserably cold and damp, and the air was full of sooty smoke. Indoors it was hardly more cheerful. Coal rationing kept the temperature low, and there was no escape from the draughts of winter. My father's death still affected the atmosphere of the household. I tried to get on with my Braille and typing, with some help from Miss Oakley, the local home-teacher for the blind. In between times I reflected on the year just ending, and thought about the year ahead.

Thanks to modern medicine and good nursing, I was still alive. I was now engaged to be married to Nancey, which meant that I would not face the future completely alone. My present circumstances might not be too rosy, nor could my hopes and expectations be very high, but since my injury I was beginning to learn new lessons in living, and as I came into contact with my contemporary St Dunstaners who were practical models of guts and determination, I was encouraged to go forward.

5

I spent the dying minutes of 1945 in Bury town centre. As the clock struck midnight the centre of the town erupted into a mass of noise; factory hooters and church bells mingled with the cheering of the crowds of people around me. This was the first New Year's Eve celebration after the end of the war, and everyone seemed determined to forget the bleak war years, and revive the pre-war custom of welcoming the New Year with a big party. My sister and her future husband had persuaded me to join the revellers, thinking it would lift my spirits if I could get alongside the bustling crowds. Under normal circumstances I probably would have enjoyed the celebrations, but I was in no real mood to participate. My father's recent death still affected me, and my blindness only emphasised my separation from normal life. My dependence on other people on this kind of occasion was also something I had not yet got used to. Had I been able to see I would have been glad to meet up with old friends again, to wish them a happy New Year, but now I could not react spontaneously to what was going on. In the midst of that excited crowd I realised, more than I had done previously, that I was a different kind of person in so many ways. I could no longer share in their exuberance. On similar occasions in the past, I too would have been one of the crowd, but now there was a gap between me and the people around me and I felt powerless to bridge it.

Not many days later another tragedy struck the family, and the extent of my inadequacy struck me with even more severity. It was my sister Peggy's 21st birthday, and the family was arranging a celebration. My mother had made an early start; the room had been swept and dusted and a cheerful fire was burning in the grate. I was in my father's chair by the window listening to the wireless. My sister was opening her presents and cards. My elder brother Fred, a 'Bevan boy', who had been on night-shift in the pit, was asleep in the front room next door. My mother was busy in the kitchen.

Just after 10 o'clock a terrifying, blood-curdling scream came from my grandmother's bedroom upstairs. My grandmother had been dressing by the warmth of an electric fire, when her nightdress had caught alight. My mother rushed to the foot of the stairs, where she saw my grandmother coming out of her room covered in flames. The screams roused Fred, who leapt upstairs, half-clothed. He managed to smother the flames and put out the fire. My grandmother was still alive but she was very badly burned. An ambulance came within minutes and she was taken to Bury Infirmary. My mother and brother were with her when she died later that day.

In the midst of all this panic and noise everyone, except me, seemed to be able to do something to help. I could only sit in my chair completely useless. I realised that if I had attempted to do anything I would have been more of a hindrance than a help. It was one of the worst days of my life, and far more traumatic for me than my close encounter with death 12 months before. It was my sense of utter helplessness, as much as the effect of my grandmother's death, which affected me, similar to my feelings when my father died. To feel redundant is a common experience for many disabled people.

The greatest sadness I feel about my grandmother today is that she was never called 'Grandma', by any of her four grandchildren, and I often wonder if this also affected her. To us she was always Auntie Emma. My grandmother was a teenage unmarried mother, and my mother was brought up as her younger sister to avoid the disapproval of the day. Nevertheless, she had a great bond with her grandchildren. She did not stint her affection for us. She was kind and generous, and well-respected by everyone who knew her.

She and my grandfather (Uncle Abraham) were married to each other eventually, and lived happily together for over 25 years, until my grandfather died in his mid-70s. I have vivid recollections of our holidays at their cottage home in Littleborough just below the craggy Pennines when we spent exciting times clambering about on the steep hills and visiting Hollingworth Lake. I shall never forget the time I was swept off my feet by a cow's tail into the stinking slurry whilst I was watching the cows being milked on Calvert's farm next to where my grandmother lived, and she had the job of cleaning me up. I now possess my grandfather's rosewood bureau, a permanent memento of them both. As a child I was fascinated by its intricate compartments and small drawers which always seemed to contain plenty of silver threepenny bits which were given to us on our visits. My grandfather was the cashier in one of the cotton mills owned by his brother Jack. He was our 'rich relation'! Now 'Auntie Emma' was gone, and all that was left was a collection of happy childhood memories.

I was so numbed by this latest tragedy that I began to lose interest in life. My grandmother's tragic death occurred only six weeks after that of my father, while I was still trying to come to terms with the devastating loss of my sight. Nothing seemed worthwhile just then and what inner reserves I had were being dissipated in self-pity and morbid introspection.

Provisional arrangements had been made for me to start my rehabilitation training at St Dunstan's in February. Before things were settled, the civilian Home Teacher, Miss Oakley, invited me to meet Mr Maurice Tomlinson, Director of Education for Bury. Throughout my schooldays the presence of this tall, silver-haired man with his ruddy complexion, carrying a black Homburg hat, had struck fear and awe in me, but face to face in his office he was simply a kind and welcoming human being, unstinting with his time and advice. He was obviously disappointed when I discussed the idea I had had about poulty farming. He thought that I should be attempting something more demanding, but at that time, poultry farming was the extent of my vision. Apart from the fact that I had no academic qualifications, I had considered a life in the countryside after the war, even before I lost my sight. Maurice Tomlinson was not the first person to think that I should be thinking about alternatives; Rev Norman

Priestley had seen me as a possible youth leader. Their confidence in me was far greater than the confidence that I had in myself. Their ambition for me seemed far too impracticable and unrealistic.

I was not a happy person when I left home on a bright cold February morning to begin my training at St Dunstan's in Church Stretton. On this occasion a member of the British Legion acted as my escort. We arrived at Stretton at lunchtime just as the trainees were finishing their morning sessions and returning to their quarters. The centre of the town was crowded with people; such was the impression I had from the noise and bustle going on around me. Stretton had been a quiet little town in the Shropshire countryside, until the coming of St Dunstan's in 1941 when hundreds of blinded ex-servicemen and women began to invade the town to start their rehabilitation training. My escort remarked, 'There are blind men everywhere - I have never seen so many white sticks in my life.' Once he had reported to the reception desk, and found me a seat in the waiting room he had completed his task; I was now the responsibility of St Dunstan's. Left alone whilst the office staff found someone to look after me, I began to wonder again what the future held. In those few moments I felt isolated and alone. I was in a strange environment, and out of contact with familiar voices. If I had decided, at that point, to change my mind about my training – a thought which had occurred to me – I had no means of escape.

As I sat there waiting for something to happen I was unable to move about freely to familiarise myself with my surroundings. I was miserable and anxious, and the chilliness of the day only emphasised my sense of isolation and unreality. I had arrived at an inconvenient moment, as most of the staff had gone for lunch. I had anticipated a formal interview and much form-filling before I was admitted, but instead I was informed that I would be going to 'Longmynd', whatever that might be. I was surprised to find that my arrival had been expected; I was led out to a waiting car, and driven by a young lady for about five minutes along a twisting, climbing path.

When the car came to a stop, she announced that we had arrived at Longmynd, one of the hotels in the Church Stretton area taken over by St Dunstan's in 1941 to meet the need for extra accommodation.

Lunch was already being served in the dining-room when I arrived. The matron of St Dunstan's, Miss Dorothy Payne, and Miss Davidson, the matron of Longmynd, welcomed me to the house and to the training centre. I felt a bit better as I was taken to a seat at the dining table. A cheerful voice on my left announced himself as Les White, one of the Braille teachers. A foreign accented voice across the table introduced himself as Frank, a Dutch ex-merchant seaman. Other voices came at me from different angles, interspersed with jokes and wisecracks. This cross-talk and badinage was a sign of welcome, which made it easy for me to join in the friendly banter. I quickly learned to identify some of the voices of my table companions. Les White, the senior St Dunstaner, was at the head of the table, and an obvious target for much of the ribaldry.

I began to learn a bit more about St Dunstan's in my first hours. It was all bewildering and confusing to start with: knowing what to do and what not to do, and who I had to approach for my different needs. It seemed to be a well-regulated pattern of life. There was a weekly programme of events and activities, but there was little variation in the daily routine: morning tea at 6.30, breakfast at 8.45, lessons from 9.30-12.30, and lunch, preceded by grace, at 1.00.

I learned, too, that my adjustment to reality was now only beginning. Being surrounded by many strange voices took some getting used to, especially when several conversations were going on simultaneously. Bumping into inanimate objects and apologising for doing so brought some humour into our lives. It was easy to forget that most of the people around were also blind, and that moving about too silently or carelessly might cause a spillage or a more serious mishap – it was a matter of trial and error. Sometimes I was the culprit, and at other times I was the victim. I made many blunders and mistakes before I got things right, but at the same time I was learning greater independence and self-reliance.

I had not been at Longmynd many days before I realised that the chief meeting point in a St Dunstan's establishment is 'the lounge', and that the focal point of 'the lounge' is 'the desk'; I believe it is still so today. The lounge was staffed continuously from 8.30 in the morning until 9.30 in the evening by the Lounge Sister or her deputy. 'The desk' provided the vital link between the individual and all the other departments of St Dunstan's. It was the place where letters were handed in to be posted, and from which incoming mail was distributed, where arrangements and most internal transactions took place, and also where advice could be sought about almost any problem or difficulty.

The next morning I was taken to see Air Commodore Dacre, the commandant of St Dunstan's. It was a brief meeting - I was given some information about the workings of St Dunstan's and presented with a timetable of lessons. As well as Braille and typewriting there were optional lessons in simple bookkeeping, current affairs, carpentry and a range of handicrafts. My programme comprised Braille, typing, carpentry, bookkeeping, current affairs and rug-making.

The next morning I joined the other trainees in the entrance hall to be taken for my first training session. The training was carried on at various locations in the village, housed in an assortment of buildings, including adapted army Nissen huts. We set off for our classes in twos and threes, linked together and accompanied by a VAD, and we took the private path to the village. It was steep, and a guide-wire had been fitted for when we were moving about unaccompanied. The end of the path was marked by a wicket-gate, before reaching a busy road near the market square. In the village we dispersed to our respective tutors to start work. At first, it was difficult to get to the scattered venues unaided, but after a little practice I even managed to find my way in the general direction of the village and Longmynd.

My day started with a double period in the 'chippy shop' – the carpentry training room. It was upstairs in the Maltings, an old brewery. Frank Ralph, a first world war St Dunstaner, was in charge, and without any delay he took me to the bench, complete with drawer and tools, which I was to use until the completion of my training. He introduced me to the other trainees and showed me samples of their work: beautifully made articles, a simple letter-rack, knife-box, tea tray, and even table lamps and cigarette boxes. He tried to assure me that within six or seven weeks I would be producing similar pieces of work, but I was sceptical. However, Frank's assessment was correct – I made each of the models in turn, and some of them are still in use today, more than 50 years later.

After my carpentry class, another VAD appeared to deliver me to my next class – 40 minutes' Braille instruction. I was already beginning to notice that VADs seemed to appear spot on cue, like genies appearing out of green smoke. I had to wait for a few minutes just inside the Nissen hut until my new teacher was ready for me. I could hear the constant clicking and tinkling of several Braille writing machines in use, and hesitant voices reading aloud to their tutors from Braille texts. I had no idea how many pupils there were in that room – possibly 10 or more – all of them at different stages of mastering Braille on a one-to-one basis. Now, here I was, about to join the large number of my fellow St Dunstaners who had passed this way before me.

My teacher was Miss Ramshaw, the senior Braille teacher and she seemed pleasantly surprised to discover that I already knew a bit about Braille. Even so, I had a considerable distance to go in learning and using the complete system; Grade 1 was comparatively simple but Grade 2 in 'inter-point' Braille was more complicated. There were small inducements for reaching higher levels of proficiency. In my eagerness to complete my preliminary training, I achieved the first reading test before the end of the term.

After my first Braille lesson, a small group of trainees were gathered for a current affairs/English discussion, under the supervision of Mr Stanners, an Oxford don seconded to the St Dunstan's training establishment as an educational advisor. These small groups provided an opportunity to keep up to date with the important matters of the day, and to develop self-expression. So ended my first morning as a new boy. It had been like going back to school, with organised set periods of lessons.

The afternoon started in the typing room with Miss Timiss, one of the typing teachers. I was glad to resume my typing instruction. Much had happened since it was interrupted. As an incentive to become a proficient typist and complete the course, the student was presented with a portable typewriter on permanent loan. Passing the typing test was my first accomplishment.

The last two periods were spent in one of the handicraft classes learning rug-making. This was not as demanding mentally as Braille and typing, but still required concentration. There were several options in addition to rug-making, including hand-weaving, mat-making, leather-work and basket-making. I opted for rug-making for practical reasons: as Nancey and I were getting married later that year, making rugs seemed a useful thing to do. I began by making a small rug of doormat size in a single colour, and progressed to make a large multicoloured one. I was first given a small piece of canvas and a few skeins of wool, which had to be rolled into balls before being cut into short lengths. The wool was wound round a wooden gauge and cut into lengths by running a razor-blade along a groove in the gauge. This was a simple and relaxing hobby, but I had to be careful in using the razor-blade and finding the right hole in the canvas without splitting it. Tying each knot was a laborious process, but the result was satisfying.

Our routine was relieved by a varied programme of activities and diversions. The weekly dance, with the trainees' own band, was always popular, and tuition was available if needed. I could also have been taught to play a musical instrument, had I been so inclined. There were also regular concerts in the main hall. Walking and tandem-riding were available for the fit and energetic and there was no shortage of entertainment in the local hostelries for those who sought it. Invitations to social functions came from local service and civilian organisations.

By Easter I had completed my basic training, and my thoughts now turned towards my future occupation. My training was a time of readjustment from near total dependence to a modest degree of independence; from a sense of insecurity to a measure of self-confidence. Listening to the successes and achievements of my contemporary St Dunstaners, I was astonished by the extensive range of occupations, business enterprises and professions into which they had ventured. Many of my fellow trainees, however, were also being trained to work in open industry as capstan-lathe and machine operators and following these successful placements there was a demand for more recruits. The prospect of being recruited for training in industry caused me some anxiety, not because I was afraid of dirtying my hands, but because I was concerned about the effect of the constant noise on my head injury. My mother suggested that I might consider shopkeeping, but if I had accepted this idea it would have jeopardised my opportunity to train in poultry farming, which Nancey and I had set our minds on. We had dreamed about the future on our own smallholding, but it was by no means certain that our dreams could be realised.

Poultry farming came under the country life department of St Dunstan's, and I would have to satisfy the controlling authority that I had the motivation and aptitude for this kind of work. They also wanted to know about Nancey's interest in the subject, so that she too would be acquainted with what was involved. We were then invited to St Dunstan's headquarters in London, where an interview had been arranged with Mr Ferguson, the Superintendent of the country life department and the Chief Welfare Officer.

The training consisted of a one-year course, which would include all the aspects of poultry farming – breeding, hatching and rearing, as well as some tuition about other small livestock. We learned before we left for home that I had been accepted for this training course.

6

My hopes for the future had brightened with the news that I had been accepted for training on the country life course. As I approached London on my way to South Mimms to start the course I was in a much more optimistic frame of mind than I was when I first went to Church Stretton to begin my initial training a few months earlier. My prospects for the future were now much better than I had once dared to hope, and many of my earlier fears had evaporated. There were still frustrations and hang-ups associated with my blindness, but I was encouraged by my achievements so far in reading and writing Braille, and by my competence in touch-typing, and other skills which had seemed impossible only a few weeks before.

The training farm was a 14-acre smallholding on the edge of South Mimms in Hertfordshire, with the grandiose name of 'The Grange'. South Mimms was then a small village at the junction of the A1 and A6 trunk roads, about 20 miles north of London, and about five miles from St Albans. The Grange stood at the end of a mile-long, badly rutted country lane and would be my address for the next ten months. I had been met off the train at Euston station by one of the St Dunstan's official cars and delivered to The Grange, still wondering about my ability to cope with my new training.

Just outside the front door there was a large, disused ornamental goldfish pond which served as a mini-roundabout at the top of the drive. There were two or three shallow steps up to the front door of the main building. Inside the entrance hall with its bare, polished, wooden floor, every sound seemed to echo, making the building seem empty and cold. In fact, just then the house was almost empty, having only four occupants - two students, and Mr and Mrs Cooper, the housekeeper and her husband, who assisted her. I was introduced to my two fellow students when they returned to the house from the evening feeding of the poultry, and over the evening meal they began to put me in the picture about the daily routine at The Grange. They prepared me for some of the snags and hazards I was likely to encounter, and gave me a few tips about coping with them. I was glad of their friendly advice.

The next morning when I donned my new dungarees and stepped into my new gumboots I felt that I was once again part of the British working community. I left my shoes in the front porch as my colleagues were doing, to avoid the wrath of the housekeeper. The entrance hall was the main thoroughfare for the students going to and from the working area, and Mrs Cooper was not pleased if her floors were soiled by dirt from the farm. This meant changing our footwear each time we came in and out, from gumboots to shoes and vice versa. Before making my hesitant way down to the range of outbuildings where the poultry food was stored and prepared, I put some identification marks on my gum-boots - short pieces of string with three small knots in the eyeholes - so that I could distinguish them from those of my colleagues when they were lined up on the doorstep in the porch.

Alongside the drive, nearer to the entrance gate and the lodge, there was a range of farm buildings, loose boxes, stables, chick-rearing sheds, workshops, and a foodstore. Close by was a garage for at least four cars which in my time accommodated some of the farm implements. Above the garage there was accommodation for a chauffeur. These rooms were taken over later by the Braille teacher, when the need for Braille instruction increased. The housekeeper and her husband had their own private quarters, and there was also a small flat which married couples could occupy for one or two weeks during the training year, enabling the wives to participate in those parts of the course where some sighted assistance was necessary.

The first signs of life in the morning came from the housekeeper's room. When we heard the clinking of teacups followed by the opening and closing of doors, we knew that Eddie, the housekeeper's husband, would soon be appearing with the early morning tea. Primed with this hot drink, we were ready to whistle our way down the drive to begin our day's work. Before mixing our quota of hot poultry mash all the pop-holes had to be opened up to let the birds out to scratch and forage in the grass. Mr Russell (Tich) the farm manager, was usually already at work when we arrived. We located the food store using a system of markers and guide-wires, or by following the sound of clanging buckets. 'Nanny', the farm goat, with her constant plaintive bleating in the loose box next door, could also give us our bearings. Most of my blind colleagues who came to The Grange could also identify the various buildings by using their sense of smell, but as I was deprived of this faculty I could not do this.

After a day or so, there was no difficulty in reaching the food store and the other farm buildings, but it was a bit more tricky finding one's way round the large field where the poultry houses were arranged in rows with almost military precision. This, too, though, was mastered after a few weeks' practice.

There were guide-wires to the various blocks of poultry houses and runs which were absolutely essential at first; to deviate from them could be disastrous. It was easy enough to find oneself wandering off course into the open field until spotted by a sighted member of staff. We each developed our own technique for coping with this and how to avoid colliding with stationary and moving obstacles. As the number of students increased it was essential to give some audible signal of one's presence when moving about the farm, especially on the soft grass in gumboots. Most of us carried a small stick with which we could tap on the wire fences to warn our blind colleagues of our presence, or, if we were pushing a wheelbarrow or carrying a bucket in each hand, we announced our presence with a shout or whistle. Even so there were frequent mishaps and spillages, when heaps of manure or poultry food would be strewn across the paths. We were not always successful in avoiding less savoury contents of barrows. It was no joke falling hands first into a heap of manure, but it was always treated as such by everyone except the unfortunate victim.

There was much more to learn about poultry farming than I had originally imagined in my romantic pipedreams. The course was intensive and thorough, covering all aspects of country life and the management of a smallholding. We studied breeding and incubating; rearing and housing, as well as the common diseases of poultry. The course also included some useful carpentry instruction when we were taught how to make feeding troughs, gates and other equipment, and how to carry out repairs with safety.

People on the course were motivated and enthusiastic, and we all seemed to take for granted the successful outcome of our training. As far as we knew, all that was expected of us was that we had gained sufficient competence to manage our own small business, and had sufficient confidence to launch out on our own. There were no formal examinations but we had, of course, to satisfy the authorities of St Dunstan's of our credentials and capabilities before we could count on their support. All those training with me during my time had some previous knowledge and experience of dealing with poultry, and other livestock on a small scale, which made us quite a useful self-help group. We picked up many helpful hints and tips from one another, and many of these homespun ideas were often applied in the running of the training farm. We were also able to make constructive suggestions during the weekly lectures, which were appreciated by the superintendent and the farm manager.

It was the height of the rearing season when I arrived at The Grange in late spring, and it would be another 12 months before I could participate in the rearing of large numbers of newly-hatched chicks. The pullets which had been hatched in late February and early March were maturing nicely in the rearing pens, ready to replace the laying stock which were then coming to the end of their first laying season. It was a new experience for me to be involved with large numbers of poultry, and quite a contrast to the couple of dozen in my father's hen pen near the terraced house where we lived in Bury. Going into a poultry run for the first time, with so many lively hens at one's feet, was almost overpowering. They seemed perpetually hungry no matter what time of day. It was worst when you entered a run with buckets of food. Hens would be flying everywhere, perching on the buckets, on your arms and shoulders, and even on your head when you were bending over trying to find the feeding troughs; a lot of feed was spilled.

In due course, when there were more trainees, we were each given our own block of houses to manage, which created an element of friendly competition between us. We had to measure, mix and prepare the food and look after the routine cleaning and pest control, and of course, collect the eggs. We were responsible for opening and closing the pop-holes on our own section each morning and night to keep out foxes, rodents and other vermin.

A week or so before Christmas our daily routine was changed to allow us to tackle another part of our training: the preparation of poultry for Christmas dinners. First, the birds had to be killed and plucked, and this was done in one of the spare loose boxes. After a brief demonstration by Mr Russell, who showed us how it was possible for a fowl to be plucked clean in a matter of minutes, we were each given a carcass to work on, but it was not surprising that we took much longer than that on our first attempts. Before long we were swamped in a sea of feathers, and even after an hour at the job none of us had completely stripped the bird we had been given to pluck. By the time we had completed this we were even colder than the poor carcasses we had been dealing with, and the discarded feathers had been transferred to us, clinging to our overcoats and hats until we looked like animated snowmen.

We then had to learn how to 'dress' the carcasses. The birds were hung for two or three days in cold conditions until we were ready to start the disembowelling process in another ice-cold loose box which had been suitably prepared for the purpose. We were each supplied with a small, sharp boning knife, a trussing needle and a ball of twine, and allotted a place at a table where we were carefully supervised, both for our own sakes and to prevent us from damaging the carcasses. In spite of the apparent danger in this practice, I am pleased to say that the only spilt blood came from the lifeless birds. Appreciation of my own performance came from Nancey's mother when I presented her with an oven-ready Christmas dinner as I arrived in Workington for the Christmas break.

By this time I had completed two-thirds of my training, but there was still much more to learn before the end of the Easter term when I was due to leave and set out in search of a suitable smallholding of my own. As yet I did not know much about breeding and hatching, or the rearing of baby chicks under artificial conditions using incubators and brooders. When we returned after the holiday this was the next part of the training to be attempted, and it proved to be one of the most interesting and demanding parts of the course.

We were also introduced to other aspects of agriculture and horticulture which might become possible for us to try once we had our own place. The large kitchen garden gave us scope to try our hand at digging, weeding and the cultivation of vegetables and other plants.

Nanny, a large, white Sanaan dairy goat provided me with the opportunity to get some experience at keeping goats. She was characteristically temperamental and particular about who she allowed to milk her. After a little coaxing she did allow me to milk her after a fashion, but no one cried over the milk I spilt when Nanny overturned the milking pail. My comrades did shed some real tears but they were tears of raucous laughter at my expense. However, Nanny and I reached a better understanding before I left The Grange.

The management of pigs was more straightforward. Their requirements were simple, and they thrived as long as their food appeared on time, and they were adequately bedded with clean straw. I did not intend to keep more than two or three pigs at a time, so the instruction I received was sufficient to enable me to take care of a few weaners and fatteners without too much bother.

My time at The Grange was, for me and those closest to me, a time of transformation and transition. In fact the immediate postwar years were the same for most people. Whilst I was being re-equipped to take my place in the community once again, after my traumatic experience and rehabilitation, the country, too, was engaged in the reconstruction of homes, towns and cities, and the rebuilding of lives after the consequences of war. The family home which I had left to join the army in 1939 had been sold and my mother had gone into business on her own.

The change from war to peace was symbolically marked by victory parades and celebrations in June 1946; Nancey was spending a few days of her annual holidays at The Grange at the time, which gave us the chance to join the excited crowds in London. We had a meal at Lyons Corner House at Marble Arch, sharing a table with a young RAF corporal and his German bride who had arrived in the country.

It was a day of noise and bustle, with military bands, dancing and singing. No doubt there were those who had real cause for rejoicing, but the thought occurred to me, 'How much did this façade mask personal grief and sorrow?' I was glad that I was able to be in the capital on this memorable occasion, but as the sound of cheerful music filled the air I could not forget my comrades who had died in Burma, and those who would be mourning them today. At the same time I was conscious that, whilst I had survived the physical battles, I still had a personal fight on my hands, and persistent inner conflicts to conquer.

An event even more significant to me than the victory celebrations took place on the 14th September in John Street Methodist Church in Workington; the day of my marriage to Nancey, and undoubtedly the most important change I was to make. The date had been arranged shortly after my return from the Far East, and as training in the Christmas term had already begun, I was granted a week off for the wedding. Everyone remarked on the beautiful appearance of the bride. It was a modest ceremony, with 50 or 60 family and friends present. The reception was no less intimidating for me than the wedding ceremony; apart from the speech I was expected to make, there was the perplexity of identifying the voices with their distinctive Cumbrian accents, many of which I was hearing for the first time. There seemed to be an endless stream of aunts, uncles and cousins whose voices I could not recognise.

The small guest house beside Loweswater where we spent the first few days of our marriage, by coincidence, had the same name as the training farm at South Mimms. Even for our honeymoon, I could not escape entirely from The Grange! By choice, we spent our time revisiting a few of the beauty spots of the Lake District. Even without my eyesight it was possible to absorb the atmosphere of the landscape which was in complete contrast to some of my earlier visits to the area in steel helmet and battledress, playing soldiers in military manoeuvres. Then it was back to the other Grange, as guests of the Russell's, to finish off the honeymoon and then to get on with my training.

Nancey gave up her job at the Trustee Savings Bank at the end of the year, and we returned to South Mimms together after the Christmas holidays to complete my course. The winter of 1947 was one of the most severe on record, and even before we got back to South Mimms the ice and snow had set in, and they remained for several weeks. Working outside in the arctic weather tested our enthusiasm for the job. The freezing temperature meant additional work for the trainees: keeping the drinking water free from ice, and clearing away piles of snow.

There was also the problem of moving about without some of the usual points of reference which the snow had covered. For the first two weeks back at The Grange Nancey and I occupied the flat in the house, and discovered some of its shortcomings, particularly its inadequate central heating system. The single radiator was barely warm at the best of times, and it became even colder whenever hot water was drawn off anywhere in the house. Each morning the windows inside were covered with ice. Under such circumstances our single, army-style beds were our greatest comfort. After our allocated two weeks Nancey found digs with one of the cottagers in the village. She was a spinster with an elderly mother and an ancient Airedale dog with bad breath and an incessant appetite. Our domestic arrangements were not ideal; me at The Grange and Nancey over a mile away in the village with snow lying thick on the ground between us. Eventually, it was agreed that I could live out with Nancey some of the time, and come in early each morning for my work on the farm. Whichever way we worked it, Nancey had considerable distances to walk each day, escorting me to and from The Grange. The least we could say was that the extra exercise did us no harm.

My hopes and expectations, which had attracted me to the country life course originally, had not diminished as Nancey and I prepared to leave South Mimms. Everything seemed to be going the way we had planned, and I was now ready to move on. I had come to The Grange as a bachelor; I was leaving it as a married man with a pregnant wife.

The coldest east winds of March were still gusting across the meadows as we said our good-byes to colleagues and staff. I had already discussed my intentions and plans with the country life Superintendent, and from now on I was on the lookout for that ideal smallholding where I could begin to apply my acquired knowledge and experience of the past 12 months. My toolbox and the appliances I had made would remain at the farm until they could be forwarded to wherever we might find a home. The cockerels out in the runs signalled our departure with continuous echoing calls, and Nanny gave us a farewell bleat as we passed her shed. We headed for the north to meet the changes and challenges of the future.

7

At this stage we were a homeless couple with a baby due to be born in a few months' time. This, however, did not strike either of us until we were comfortably settled in the train heading for Manchester. We were on our way to spend Easter with my mother in Bury before starting the long search for a suitable smallholding, and our own dream home in the countryside.

My mother was now living at the other side of town with my sister and younger brother, in the small corner sweets and tobacco shop she had bought since I had started my training. The shop was at the end of a row of old terraced houses, and although the business was good, living space was barely adequate for two extra adults. In any case, we were eager to get on with our search for somewhere to live and work.

If things were going to work out as we had planned, this probably would be my only opportunity for some time to revisit some of the favourite haunts and locations of my childhood and youth. Nancey, of course, was in unfamiliar territory in Bury. All she had seen of the town until now had been the grimy industrial areas, with their smoking factory chimneys; the dirty Bury/Bolton canal, and the polluted River Irwell. I wanted to prove to her that Lancashire had much more to offer than the proverbial clogs and shawl image, and that there was much more to see than noisy cotton mills and greasy engineering workshops. I wanted to show her that Bury and its surroundings had its own particular beauty and attractiveness. Contrary to Lancashire's reputation as a county of soot and grime, there was still plenty of open farmland, green fields and pleasant country walks over moorland and craggy hillsides.

The day after we arrived was Good Friday. On that day, as long as I can remember, people in Bury have been drawn to Holcombe Hill, in a kind of pseudo-religious pilgrimage. The hill is not very high by comparison with some of the lakeland fells of Nancey's native Cumberland, but it is a sufficient climbing challenge to many Lancastrians on this special day. A long interval had elapsed since I was last in these parts, and I wondered if I would be able to recall the route now that I could no longer see. Nancey was entirely dependent on me as her guide, and she was relying on my memory to take her along obscure paths, over stiles and bridges, before we got to our destination. I was surprised how easy it was to find our way. Given a few clues and descriptions of the passing landscape I knew exactly where I was, and this gave Nancey a bit more confidence in me as I led her along barely recognisable pathways. I had deliberately taken a circuitous route for our ramble, as this would take in more of the scenic landscape, and some of the quainter Lancashire villages.

Holcombe Hill proved just a little too much for Nancey in her pregnant state, not because of the steep climb, but the thought of what might happen if we were knocked off our feet by any of the youngsters who were hurling themselves down the hill in a roly-poly fashion, just as I had done at their age. Descending the slippery grassy slopes might also have proved tricky so it was just as well that we did not make the attempt. We covered several miles that day, mostly on foot, and completed our trip on the bone-shaking electric train which took us from Holcombe Brook to Bury.

This episode was something of a triumph, and we congratulated ourselves on the day's adventure. Nancey had enjoyed the strenuous exercise without any disadvantage to herself or the baby, and I had managed to navigate a circular tour on part of my native ground without serious mishap. The jaunt had certainly revived thoughts of earlier days, and Nancey had seen something of the bleak grandeur of my own county. The aroma of fresh baking met us as soon as we entered the house; a pot of tea and home-made chocolate buns revived us.

There were other similar adventures before we left for Cumberland, but to my chagrin, not all were as successful as our Good Friday outing. Nancey was not always pleased when I took her through smelly farmyards puddled with slurry, or under boundary fences tangled with barbed wire. Such incidents were rare, but when they occurred my ego and self-confidence were reduced to proper proportions.

We hoped to make our home somewhere between our own respective home grounds in Cumberland and Lancashire. This would be convenient for family visits, and for when help was urgently needed. This area was also the home of several well-known poultry breeding and hatching establishments, from which I could obtain reliable replacement stock when necessary. The search for a suitable smallholding began for me and my colleagues whilst we were training at South Mimms, co-opting relatives and friends to be on the look-out for likely properties. Nancey's parents agreed to put us up whilst we got on with our search. They may have thought differently once we started to clutter the house with second-hand furniture, carpets and other household goods. Like most newly-weds at that time, we were keen to pick up any good second-hand articles, even before we knew where we would be living.

We were always on the lookout, too, for useful things for the smallholding, and I could not resist going to farm sales to see what I might get hold of cheaply, even though I was expecting to start up with new poultry houses. The local auctioneers were always very helpful to me. I may say in one case, almost too helpful. Some poultry houses were being sold off on one of the properties in which we were interested. Unfortunately, due to a misunder-standing with the auctioneer I got landed with a shed by mistake. Sadly, on closer inspection it was not in very good condition, but as it had to be paid for on the spot and removed as soon as possible, there was nothing I could do about it. What made things worse was that I had nowhere to store it, and had some explaining to do before my in-laws consented to let me store it in their backyard. After that experience I made sure when attending an auction sale that I was out of range of the auctioneer's glance. When we eventually moved, the household items we had collected, plus the shed, more than half filled the furniture van which carried our possessions to Lancashire.

All our efforts at house hunting seemed futile, and after weeks of searching we became desperate, wondering if we would ever find a place of our own before the baby was born. We started out with great expectations, looking for that ideal cottage in the country with roses round the door and two or three acres of land with trees and hills in the background, but the dream faded as the days went on. We had thought it would be easy enough to find such a place in the Lake District, but it was not to be. At that point, I would have accepted anything as long as it had enough land and sufficient scope for my poultry enterprise. Nancey did not altogether share my viewpoint. My reckoning was, if only we could find a place to get started, no matter how run-down or dilapidated, we could make improvements as we went on. I was prepared, like an early pioneer, to struggle on in primitive conditions until we got established. Nancey felt that we should at least have hot and cold water and other basic amenities, for when the baby came.

We were so sure that we would easily find a place in Cumberland that we booked a bed for Nancey in the maternity wing of the local hospital. However, the only places being advertised proved unsuitable even though they all sounded just right from the glowing descriptions in the newspaper advertisements. At the top of the market there were several elegant country houses for sale, with stylish suites of out-buildings, paddocks for ponies, orchards and walled kitchen gardens, which were obviously beyond our means. At the other end of the scale there were poky little hovels, portrayed as desirable country cottages. When the state of some of these places were pointed out even I began to have doubts about roughing it.

Between Easter and Whitsun Nancey and I travelled hundreds of miles by train, bus and even on foot, covering the whole area we had mapped out. Many of the places we viewed got our immediate thumbs-down without even a word with the vendors. We were in a forlorn mood by this time, wondering if we really would find somewhere to live before the baby arrived. But then we had some good news, which revived our flagging spirits. A telegram arrived from John Brady, the St Dunstan's representative, asking us to contact him immediately about a vacant property in Lancashire. When I telephoned, he told me he had spotted a property for sale in Farington, near Preston: a semi-detached house with two acres of land. If we were interested he would contact the vendor and arrange a time for us to inspect the place. John Brady met us at Preston, and took us by car for our first glimpse of The Poplars, the house which was to be our home for the next 23 years.

The only bit of Preston with which I was familiar was its railway station. Many times, during the war years as a hard-up soldier, I had used its free services' canteen on platform six, and consulted the rotating timetable as I had scurried between connections amid crowded platforms and hissing steam engines, but I had never been past the ticket barrier into the town. My last visual recollection of Preston was from a blacked-out troop train as we sped through it in the early hours of the morning on our way to embark on the troop ship, *Mataroa*, destined for South Africa and the Far East.

It was drizzling rain when we made our first visit to The Poplars. The gloomy skies did nothing to improve the landscape. For the first few miles Nancey reported that she could see nothing but houses, shops and factory chimneys; only when we were coming into Farington, over the railway bridge, was there any sign of open country. Apart from the rise over the station bridge, the road was flat, straight and uninteresting.

The Poplars stood on the right and slightly back from the road; the right-hand house of a block of three. A grass verge and ditch separated the front garden from the footpath and road. It was a typical redbrick house with some pebble-dashing, built just before the outbreak of the war; bay-windowed, with two reception rooms, kitchen, two bedrooms, a box-room and bathroom. Adjacent to the house, at the rear, there was a brick-built washhouse. A rough cart-track ran along the side of the house from the road to an old wooden barn about 30 yards beyond. This had been used as a cart-shed and stable by the previous owner. At the rear of the barn there was a large, stagnant pond, and lying round about was an old car chassis and a broken fieldgate. To the right of the cart-track was a ditch and hedge, 300 yards in length, which marked the northern boundary.

As we tramped across this bare tract of land we both realised that we would have to make a decision immediately. To delay might mean a lost opportunity to get a roof over our heads, and our search would have to continue. It was not the ideal site, but with some effort it had the makings of a small poultry farm. A stocky, elderly unshaven man with one arm showed us over the premises. He was wearing an old gaberdine mac and a battered trilby hat. Nancey thought that he was someone employed by the owner to show people round, but it turned out that he was the owner.

The Poplars was far from that idyllic cottage we had always imagined, but it was newly-decorated and ready for immediate occupation as soon as the legal formalities were completed. It was still raining when we started back, but the general atmosphere was much brighter - we now had somewhere to live. Nancey could not get home quickly enough to give the good news to the family.

8

In spite of many agitated phone calls completion of the sale was slow, and it was not until the beginning of the third week in July that we saw The Poplars again. Our arrival in our new home in Farington coincided with the annual Wakes Week when, unknown to us, the whole town appeared to close down. We discovered that all the factories, offices, and even most of the shops shut their doors for the traditional holiday week, and the whole area seemed deserted and as silent as the moon. In contrast to our earlier visit it was a blisteringly hot, cloudless day, and the sun beat down on us as we found our way to the house. On our previous visit to view the premises we had arrived by car, accompanied by a member of St Dunstan's staff; this time we were accompanied by my mother, and travelling by bus and on foot.

As yet, we did not have the keys to our new house. It had been arranged that we should collect them from the little farmhouse immediately across the road, where the previous owner had left them. As we had no means of informing them of our time of arrival, we just hoped that there would be someone around when we got there, but we need not have worried. No sooner had we opened the front garden gate, than the lady with the keys came to meet us. She introduced herself as Mrs Bilsborrow, and invited us over for a cup of tea.

As we sat chatting in the stone-flagged kitchen of the farmhouse, the sound of clog-irons in the kitchen doorway signalled the entrance of Mr Bilsborrow, who had been working outside. He was closely followed by his dog, Bess. Before long we had exchanged details about our respective families, and they had given us some background information about the area. They had already gleaned some scraps of information about this young blind man and his family who were coming to live across from them, and from the start we struck up a good working relationship. They immediately offered us help.

Little New House Farm, the home of the Bilsborrow's, was now only a small acreage; Mr Bilsborrow's also worked part-time at Leyland Motors.

Pleasant as it was to be enjoying our first contact with our new neighbours, I was eager to get across the road, and to open the door of The Poplars for the first time. As we entered the house, it seemed an age since we were last here. Everything was just as we had left it months previously. Our voices and footsteps echoed noisily through the hollowness of the empty building. Nancey described to me the view from each room in turn, whilst my mother made her own investigations. From the front bedroom she could see the meandering River Lostock just beyond Bilsborrow's farm. In the middle distance stood the towering chimney of Farington Mill, and in the background the slopes of Rivington Pike. The view from the back bedroom beyond our boundary hedge was the flat, extensively cultivated Farington Moss, which to Nancey looked dull and uninteresting in comparison to her native Cumbrian hills and valleys.

Whilst Nancey explored with her eyes, I explored with my hands and fingers the corners and crevices, the exact location of doors, windows and cupboards. This had been my first opportunity to pace the empty rooms and make a mental picture of the interior of the empty house. I was as excited as a child captivated by a new discovery. I imagined Nancey was too, as we planned the arrangement of the furniture. The next thing was to find the mains switch for the electricity supply and the taps for turning on the gas and water.

The mains for electricity was in a small cupboard near the front door, but as there were no light bulbs in the sockets, we had no means of testing it. We found the gas meter in the cupboard under the stairs, but we would be unable to cook until our gas cooker arrived and was connected. The stop-tap for the water was awkwardly situated below the pavement close to the front gate.

We lit fires in the downstairs rooms, in spite of the hot weather, to remove any lingering trace of dampness, knowing that the house had stood empty for many weeks. We had come prepared for this, bringing paper and kindling wood with us. We had had to register with a coal merchant before we moved in, and we were hoping that our allocation of coal would have been delivered as promised. Perhaps the airing of the house was not absolutely necessary, but having fires in the grates had a symbolic value, signifying the possession of our new home.

Before returning to my mother's house for the night, we took another stroll up 'the field', as we were afterwards always to call it, to get some idea of the priorities awaiting me. The most noticeable change here was that the grass, which was not much higher than a rough lawn when we were last here, had now grown to waist height, and would need to be mown before anything could be done on the land. The old wooden barn was still standing, and was obviously in need of immediate renovation. The rusty car chassis and the broken field gate still lay by the pond, which was now covered with green algae. The water looked innocent enough just then, but I realised that something would have to be done to render it safe, not only for my own sake, but for the infant we visualised would be toddling about the place within the next 12 months.

It was quiet and peaceful standing at the edge of the field on this warm summer evening with Nancey beside me. My dream of the past few years had not quite been realised, but it was there in embryo. Below the surface of my mind, as I chewed a long length of grass, I was sorting out the problems to be tackled in transforming this bare two-acre field into the model small poultry farm of my imagination.

I was conscious that, for the past two and a half years, I had barely been more than a passenger in society, being carried along by a number of social agencies. Starting with my helpless state on the banks of the Irrawaddy, I had been more or less dependent on other people for all my needs; for too long I had been someone else's responsibility: army colleagues, doctors, nurses, and all the ancillaries, the training staff at St Dunstan's, to say nothing of my dependence on family and friends alike. Prior to the incident which deprived me of my eyesight, I had enjoyed a position of leadership and responsibility: now I was at one of those important junctures in life, such as leaving school or joining the army. I was on the verge of a new beginning; once again I was on the move, not from dependence to complete independence, but into a position where I could make my own contribution to society, and where I could support my wife and family.

We were back at The Poplars shortly after nine o'clock the next day, this time in our working clothes, ready to begin shaping our new existence. We were expecting Nancey's brother Ken to arrive from Workington on his motor bike to lend a hand. Two delivery vans were also due to arrive that morning with some of our furniture and other articles; one from Bury, and one from London. The rest of furniture would not come until the following day. For the first hour or so it was almost as quiet and peaceful as the previous evening, just as may be expected in a rural area. Then, suddenly, things began to happen, and from then on the turbulence went on for weeks. First, we heard the clatter of Mr Bilsborrow's clogs as he appeared round the side of the house, offering to mow the field for me. He was soon back with two of his sons, Frank and Jack. They brought their old mowing-machine pulled by their horse, and disappeared up the field to make a start on the hay-making.

Shortly afterwards we were thrown into a state of near panic when a young uniformed telegraph boy delivered a message from the poultry breeder in Carlisle, urging me to take immediate delivery of the 200 growing pullets which were on order. Originally, we were expecting delivery in May, when the pullets were eight weeks old, and now the supplier was desperate to get the stock off his hands, not only because the pullets were consuming too much poultry food but because he did not have room for them.

It was a critical situation for us both, and I felt completely powerless as I had neither poultry houses nor poultry food on the site. It made matters worse, not being able to contact Carlisle by phone. The nearest public telephone box, we were told, was almost a mile away. I was in a complete quandary, as I could not expect Nancey to go rushing off to telephone in her condition, and I was on unfamiliar territory and had no idea how to get to the telephone. It was only when Nancey's brother arrived, some two hours later, that I was able to phone a message through to the supplier, although I was unable to offer him an immediate solution.

It was a worrying situation to be in. I had been frustrated before when I had been unable to take direct action because of my blindness, but they had been nothing in comparison to my present predicament. I was in a strange and new location and I was hardly known by the people amongst whom we had come to live. I was being pressed to take delivery of stock for which I could not make adequate provision, and at the same time I was trying to cope with all the domestic goings-on of the first day in a new house. As I saw it, I was now a small businessman, and I was supposed to make decisions and get things organised. It was something of a test at the start of my enterprise; if I could not handle this sort of a problem at the start, how was I going to manage when things got properly underway?

Whilst I was still considering how best to solve the issue of my pullets a van drew up at the front gate with the items from Bury. Although we were glad for the early delivery of our goods, it only added to the confusion and chaos that was gradually building up. We needed some help with the unloading and a place had to be found for everything in turn. Nancey decided where the cooker had to go but it still had to be connected, so Ken and I set off to phone the gas company hoping that the connection could be made very soon. But, because it was the annual wakes week, they would not be able to come until later in the week at the earliest, so we would have to manage all our hot meals on the old gas ring we had brought from Nancey's mother's.

In the meantime, Nancey was trying to get on with cleaning the rooms. She was determined to have every floor scrubbed clean before carpets were laid, which was asking a lot under the circumstances. I still do not know how we accomplished it, but by some miracle we had finished the essential cleaning to her satisfaction before nightfall. That night we slept on the bare boards of the bedroom with no curtains at the windows because the van from London with its load of furniture did not arrive until the next day, but it was our home, and it was clean, and the doors were locked.

In spite of the bareness of the surroundings, it was good to be waking up in our own bedroom for the very first time. The front bedroom, in which we slept, faced almost due east, and caught the first rays of the sun, and the low-lying mist over the river promised another glorious day. The hay-makers were back on the field as soon as the dew was off the ground. We made the acquaintance of our next-door neighbours and got the usual offers of help. It was going to be another hectic day with the arrival of the other loads of furniture and equipment later on.

The rest of the furniture came as we had hoped, so at least we should have a bed to lie on that night. At teatime, a large lorry arrived unannounced with all the equipment for the farm: 12 sectional poultry houses, two store-sheds, one greenhouse, and other sundry items. The lorry driver expected the unloading to be done immediately, as he had another delivery to make that night. As pleased as I was to see all this equipment arrive, it was not exactly the most appropriate time, with the hay-making still in progress. Just then, it was a matter of an urgent call on the neighbours and dumping everything by the side of the path until I could get matters sorted out. Miraculous as it seems from this distance, by the end of the week there was some temporary housing erected for the young pullets I was expecting, but it would be some time before all the poultry houses and buildings could be arranged as I had visualised them.

Two days later, after I had sorted out a supply of poultry food, my pullets arrived from the local railway station in several crates. It was a delight to be handling my own livestock, and I felt a great sense of fulfilment as I carefully examined each bird when I lifted it from the crate. The pullets, too, seemed to enjoy their freedom as I let them flutter down from my hands to begin pecking and scratching in the chopped-straw litter on the floor of the poultry house. Handling the birds personally at this point had several advantages. Originally I had arranged to take them over at eight weeks old, but they were now twice that age. If they were sufficiently developed they could be expected to come into lay within the next eight to 10 weeks. It was obvious from their condition that they had not suffered from their journey. The smoothness of their feathers, the texture of their flesh and their bone structure were indicators that this was good healthy stock, and that each of these 200 pullets would give me a good start in business. Handling the birds individually in this way would help me to get to know my stock better. It would probably make them more docile, and also give me some idea when I may expect them to produce the first egg.

It was now a matter of putting into practice all the training I had received over the past year or so. Having a flock of 200 hens of my own to look after was very different to having my own pet hen in my father's back yard when I was only a schoolboy. I confined the pullets to the poultry house for the first couple of days, to accustom them to their feeding and roosting quarters before allowing them into the hastily erected temporary run. That first day I was going up to the poultry house about every half-hour, as quietly as I could, to ensure that everything was as it should be. The most critical time would be at dusk, the normal time of roosting, when there may be some crowding and smothering, especially as the birds had not yet got into the habit of perching. Being in a strange environment there would be a tendency for them to huddle in a corner on top of each other until they had learned to settle on the perches. To reduce this risk, I had laid some of the perches at floor level. The next morning I was up much earlier than usual, to see that everything was still all right, and to pick up my old routine, from my South Mimms days, of feeding and watering before sitting down to my own breakfast.

Enraptured as I was with my growing pullets, and the gradual transformation of my two acres of land, the anticipated birth of our first baby in October was the most important matter on our minds. We still had to get most of the essential nursery equipment: pram, cot, baby linen and other items. The cot came second-hand from Nancey's cousin. Nancey had set her mind on a new coach-built pram, and we got this from a specialist shop in town, in spite of the scarcity of such articles just after the war.

The pattern of our lives became less chaotic as the weeks passed, at least for a time. The arrival of a blind man in the district apparently aroused some interest, and people were curious about this young couple who were hoping to start a small poultry farm in their midst. It was a long time before I became familiar with the immediate locality, and gained sufficient confidence to venture beyond the farm gate by myself. It was only when I had built up a mental map of the pavements, gateways and roadside ditches and other hazards that I dared go as far as the corner shop and the postbox by myself. With the exception of our next-door neighbours and the Bilsborrows it took me longer to get to know the people around about than it did Nancey. It was surprising how self-conscious and diffident many people were in speaking to me for the first time. They seemed to regard my blindness as an impenetrable barrier to normal social relationships. It became easier as I began to recognise voices that were speaking to me, and as I became better known to the regulars, postmen, dustmen, and the various traders.

Once a start had been made setting up the poultry houses and runs, making the pond safe was the next job to be done. Someone suggested that the Leyland Motor Company may be able to help me with this to our mutual benefit. At the time they were looking for sites to dispose of their refuse sand from their main foundry at the other side of Farington, and an agreement was struck, provided that the heavily-loaded lorries could have easy access to the pond. When we had dumped the old car-chassis, and the other debris lying around, hundreds of lorry-loads of refuse-sand, amounting to several thousand tons, went up the drive and was tipped into the pond until the job was done.

The summer of 1947 was as pleasantly hot as the previous winter had been cold and miserable. Before the onset of the chilly autumn mornings, our days had settled down into a regular pattern; Nancey with her household chores, and me with my routine of feeding and watering of the poultry, and regular cleaning of the dropping-boards and poultry houses. As the weather got colder it was time to dig out my old army greatcoat and bush hat to wear around the farm. The poultry houses were now in their permanent positions, and the pullets were maturing well. I had also bought in and reared some chickens for the Christmas trade. The darker evenings gave us the chance to continue to make improvements inside the house. When Nancey was not busy knitting for the baby, she found time to fill me in with items from newspapers and poultry keeping magazines. It was this that sparked off the idea of having a dog, primarily as a guard dog, but also we thought it would be an advantage for the baby to grow up with a dog around. A breeder in Bradford was advertising Airedale/Collie cross eight-week old puppies for sale. We sent off our £2, but the first pup we were sent apparently caught a chill during the journey and died shortly after he arrived. His replacement, Kim, came to us about ten weeks before Paul was born, and he was part of the family for the next 16 years. Kim grew up with our two children. When they were babies, Kim zealously protected them as he lay beneath the pram in the front porch. As a farm dog, he also had the knack of shepherding and capturing straying hens, and viciously attacking vermin and other predators.

Nancey continued her weekly antenatal appointments for examinations and exercises. According to the doctors, the baby was due to be born on 8th October and whilst Nancey was waiting and watching for the first signs of Paul's appearance, I was looking for the first egg to be laid by my pullets. From my frequent handling of the birds at roosting time I knew that it would not be too long. There was growing excitement in both departments as we anticipated these two 'firsts' in our lives. Both events were significant milestones, but it was the egg which arrived first.

I was busy in one of the sheds on the morning it happened. There was a loud, squawking cackle from one of the poultry houses, and I hurried over to see if I could find the newly-laid egg. After some rooting around on my hands and knees in the litter I found it under the dropping-board. I picked up this small, warm egg, and, beaming with delight, took it to show Nancey.

Nancey's labour pains did not start for another week or more. It was early in the morning of Wednesday, 22nd October when she awoke me to tell me that she thought something was beginning to happen. Nancey's mother, who was sleeping in the room next door, knocked at the door to see if everything was all right. Nancey's weekend case, containing all her requirements, had been ready for weeks, and it was not long before we were all on our way to Preston Royal Infirmary in a Rolls-Royce limousine from the local taxi company. It was now a matter of waiting, and everything seemed strangely silent as Nancey's mother and I returned home to await the expected message that mother and baby were both well. We had no telephone of our own at the time, so we had to depend on our nearest neighbour with a phone to bring us the news. I was restless all day, and did not settle until late that evening, when our neighbours, Mr and Mrs Limb, called to tell us that Paul had been born at 8.30 in the evening, and that all was well.

9

I had to suppress my urge to go to the hospital immediately, and it was not until visiting time the next evening that I could hold my baby son and give my wife a hug of congratulation. It seemed an extra long time that I was standing out in the cold, along with all the other new fathers, waiting to be admitted to the maternity wing. Fathers and other visitors were not supposed to have physical contact with the babies for reasons of hygiene, but an exception was made in my case. I was a bit nervous about handling a newly-born baby for the first time, for fear that, not being able to see, I may drop him; a fear which has never entirely left me.

The next few visits helped to prepare me for what to expect when mother and baby arrived home. I could not see me being much use in the nursery routine of feeding and changing, but during my bus journeys to and from the hospital I had to work out what my role would be in the alteration to our daily routine, and to integrate this with the ongoing work with the poultry.

We arrived home in style in the same Rolls-Royce, taxied by the same lady driver. This was my first real chance to hold my baby son without feeling too self-conscious. It had been an early start that day for Nancey's mother and me preparing the house for the baby's home-coming. The carry-cot, standing in the corner of the living-room, had been warmed for its new occupant.

Having a new baby in the house, with all the accompanying noises and activity, contrasted with the relative peace and quiet which reigned before his arrival. We could now regard ourselves as a family with everything that the word implies. From now on everything had to revolve round the baby's routine, and when my mother-in-law returned home I had to take my share of the chores round the house besides tending the livestock. Nancey was now fully occupied with her nursery duties, so I could hardly expect her to do much on the farm. In any case, being a very new mother, she was preoccupied with the baby and reluctant to let him out of her sight, even for a second. Any unusual sound brought her quickly to the side of the carry-cot, and if things seemed silent for too long she was convinced there was a problem. At first we had some discussions about whether or not Baby Paul should be placed upstairs alone in the partial darkness, or whether he should stay downstairs in his carry-cot until we ourselves went to bed. After a little experimenting we discovered that everyone was more contented if the baby was allowed to be alone in the quietness, without the constant fussing of anxious parents.

There was nothing unusual about Paul's sleeping pattern, and like most other families we had our share of disturbed nights. If the disturbance was just a matter of feeding and changing, that was Nancey's department so I soon drifted back to sleep. If the peace of the night was not restored with food and attention to bodily comfort, then it was my turn to take over, pacing the bedroom floor humming either the 'Eriskay Love Lilt', or the 'Skye Boat Song'. By the time our daughter Susan was born two and a half years later I had become quite an expert. My nursing skill was used in later years when our eight grandchildren came along. These tranquillising melodies are now the traditional family 'lullabies', and should I ever be marooned on that mythical desert island one of these tunes would have to be included in my choice of music.

As we approached our first Christmas at The Poplars life became busier than ever. The pullets were now in full lay, and giving us a satisfactory return for all our labour. Each week the lorry from the egg-packing station would call to collect several cases of eggs and deliver a welcome cheque for the previous week's consignment. Small though it was, it was gratifying to be making a positive contribution towards the national food supply, and it was even more gratifying knowing that I was now making full provision for my wife and family.

From now on there was little spare time, even less than we had hoped for, especially as it got nearer to Christmas Day. There was always something to be done. When Paul was comfortably tucked away at night Nancey and I would be cleaning and packing eggs whilst we listened to the radio. This, with our occasional visits to my mother's home in Bury, was our chief relaxation. I had taken quite a lot of orders for table birds for Christmas, and these all had to be plucked and dressed. Often it would be after midnight when I returned to the house from the plucking shed, covered in feathers and numb with cold.

As this was the first Christmas in our own home, we were planning a large family gathering, with visitors from both sides of the family. It was going to be a great occasion, and Nancey had found time, somehow or other, to do all the extra preparations. I, too, was busy finishing off my first batch of Christmas chickens to be produced on the farm.

All seemed to be going well except for a spot of bother with the dining-room fire, which had been puffing the odd small cloud of smoke back into the room. As time went on it got worse, until just a few days before Christmas when it had got so bad that I sought the advice of a local builder. He considered that there was probably a fault between the back-boiler and the flue. The result was that the day before our families arrived, we had to have a new fireplace installed. Late on Christmas Eve, just before everyone appeared on the doorstep, we were still scrubbing the dining-room floor and trying to make the house presentable. In the midst of it all I had still the final chicken to dress for our own Christmas dinner.

After all this, when we re-lit the fire, smoke was still pouring down the chimney into the room as badly as ever. With groans of despair, we decided that nothing more could be done until after the holidays so we would just have to make the best of things.

In spite of the smoke-laden atmosphere and the bare plaster wall round the fireplace, there were some compensations, especially for the grandparents who could escape to other parts of the house and indulge their affections for their first grandchild. What had seemed to be our biggest problem initially, that of bedding everyone down overnight, was nothing to the one which faced Nancey when she realised that there was likely to be a shortage of vegetables at dinner. Not having cooked for a large number of people before she had underestimated the quantities she needed, and there was a slight embarrassment when the child-sized portions appeared on our dinner plates. However, no one starved; it was all taken with a good humour, and put down to excusable inexperience. The incident can still raise a smile.

We had not considered going to Workington for the New Year until Nancey mentioned it casually after our families had returned home. I agreed that this was not a bad idea as the past months, and particularly the last few weeks, had been pretty hectic. A few days away after all the upheaval would make a pleasant change. Secretly, I had a feeling that there may have been a conspiracy between Nancey and her mother, who wanted to show off the new baby to relatives and friends back home. Our good neighbours, the Bilsborrows, from across the road willingly agreed to look after things whilst we were away. The New Year's break gave us a respite, renewed our energy, and prepared us for the greater, then unknown, upheavals which lay ahead of us in the coming year.

The problem of the smoking chimney was eventually solved, but not without further inconvenience. In later months we had even worse structural problems to contend with. Nancey had been complaining for some time about a bad smell in the house, and to mask the unpleasantness she was constantly sprinkling Dettol everywhere around the place. About the same time we noticed the appearance of several patches of dampness in the downstairs rooms, which, at first, I suspected were caused by condensation due to the cold weather. But the fault persisted well into the spring, and eventually we discovered that water was lodging beneath the floorboards to a depth of over two feet, and that the ends of the joists were rotting in the walls. We then discovered that the septic tank was not working properly, and this had also been backing up under the floor of the house. For more than three months we had to live upstairs, taking all our carpets and furniture with us. The cooking still had to be carried on as usual in the kitchen, with great difficulty. During this time all the downstairs floorboards were taken up and we had to get accustomed to balancing on planks laid across the joists whilst the water was drained away, the area built up with gravel, and a concrete foundation laid.

It was a trying time for us, and although neither of us was prepared to speak it aloud, there were times when we were tempted to quit, but we had already invested too much in time, effort and money to give up at this stage. Many of our relatives and friends suggested that we should evacuate the house until the work was completed, but that was impracticable just then, with the most important period in the poultry farming year just ahead. Several day-old pullets were due to be delivered shortly, and I wanted to make sure that they had a good start. It would not have been right for me to delegate the responsibility of rearing very young chickens to anyone else. In any case, the thought had not seriously crossed my mind that anyone but myself would be doing the work around the farm in this, my first actual rearing season. In the meantime, Nancey had enough on her hands coping with a growing baby and the upheaval to our domestic routine. Fortunately, it was a dry, sunny spring, and we had plenty of offers for taking Paul out in his pram, getting him away from the dirt and the incessant noise of hammering and the grinding of the cement-mixer. I had no doubt that in time we would overcome the problems with the house, despite the present difficulties; and so we plodded on. We had overcome setbacks before, and to us this was just another one.

In March, the day-old pullets, 200 Rhode Island Reds and 200 Light Sussex from my supplier in Carlisle, were delivered to Farington railway station. These were replacements for my present stock which would be coming to the end of their first laying season in the autumn. As one of my main interests in poultry husbandry was in breeding, my aim in the early years was to build up a good foundation flock of birds from which I could select suitable breeders. I did not do any breeding or incubating in my first year, because, according to my tutors, the birds in their first laying season are too immature to be used as breeding stock. By the second year I hoped to be in a position to use my own selected birds for breeding and hatching, buying in approved stock-cockerels from reliable sources when necessary.

I was now living a very full life. If I was not attending to my enlarged flock of poultry, I was either busy in the greenhouse or trying to create a vegetable garden. Nor was I excused my share of the domestic duties. When the baby was not being wheeled out by one of our helpful neighbours, or when Nancey had to do some shopping in town, Paul would be left close by me in his pram whilst I got on with my work. This was about as much as I could manage in the nursing line at this stage, and as long as I remembered where the pram was located there was nothing much to worry about, for little Paul was either fast asleep or sitting up, fascinated by the chickens.

Before the contractors finished on the house, I got them to smarten up some other buildings on the farm. A large wooden barn, which had been used by the previous owner as a stable and coal store, had been neglected during the war, and most of the poultry houses and store-sheds which had to be erected in haste by myself and a few friends on our arrival on the premises had not been properly situated. Timber for repairs to property was still in short supply, and generally could only be obtained under license. After the men had been at work for a few days the place was transformed. The old barn had been demolished and from the reclaimed material I was presented with a modified Dutch barn and a dual purpose stable/store-shed. The poultry houses were properly lined up and arranged in a similar manner to the South Mimms layout, so that I could get round the blocks easily. I was now attracting a number of visitors and I wanted to display things at their best. I was told that my pullets, especially the Light Sussex, made a pleasant picture in their spacious runs, against the background of neatly-trimmed green grass.

After the departure of the builders I turned my attention to buying our first dairy goat. I bought Snowy, an all-white, hornless British Sanaan. Her pedigree name was 'Prestonian Snow', hence the name Snowy. As I was not interested in goat breeding, and only wanted her for providing milk for the family, I did not purchase Snowy's pedigree documents, which would have doubled her price. She was just three years old and, having recently kidded, she had an abundant supply of milk. It was evident from her high milk yield giving over a gallon a day that she was content with her new home and owner. This she did for most of her life, apart from when she was in kid. We had enough for all our household use, including butter and cheese, and some to spare for the chickens, and pigs too, when we got some. Both of our children were brought up on goat's milk, and always looked the picture of health.

For most of the time Snowy was a contented animal, but only as long as she could have her own way. She had a distinct personality with a mind of her own. It was obvious that she was not used to being tethered, and showed her disapproval of it by her continual bleating. Allowing her some freedom was the only way to keep her quiet, but this meant that I had to reinforce all the chicken runs with sheep-netting because of her back-scratching habit. She was more inquisitive that any other goat I have known, and we could have well called her Nosy instead of Snowy. If I was having a conversation with someone she had to be in on it, and would stand there nuzzling their hand or nibbling at their jacket. If she could get anywhere near the house and the door was open, it was her treat to raid the dog biscuits which were stored in the back porch. The neighbours got used to her meandering, but there was one occasion when she gave Agnes, our next-door neighbour, the fright of her life. Somehow she got through the dividing fence and into the passageway between the two houses, where Agnes used to hang out her washing. Being confronted unexpectedly, just as it was going dark, by a large white goat, she let out a scream of horror and yelled, 'B*** h***, what next!' It was even worse some time later when her daughter-in-law, Peggy, was living next door. When she was confronted with Snowy, she just yelled and fainted.

The next time Snowy was in kid I decided to buy another goat, so that we would have a continuous supply of milk, and so Queenie arrived, another Sanaan who equalled Snowy in her milk yield. She had a more placid nature than Snowy, and was not half as inquisitive. When Snowy gave birth it was twins, male and female, pure bred Sanaans. Queenie seemed as pleased as Snowy at the event, and took her share of mothering them. All the goats got on well together, with little animosity, but Snowy was undoubtedly the boss.

Snowy's kids, Dumpy and Billy, soon grew up to be as frisky and cheeky as their mother. No one would have thought so seeing them as infants, always cuddled up together, the picture of innocence. They were full of mischief from being very young. I was baffled the first time I found them cavorting round the field when I had left them safely bolted in the shed with only the top half of the door open. This happened regularly, until one day, Nancey was amazed to see them leap through the open part of the door. We discovered that they were using the walls of the shed rather like the 'Wall of Death' on a fairground, gradually gaining momentum until they were able to thrust themselves forward and leap to freedom. When they were bigger they even discovered how to manipulate the inside bolt and make their escape.

Reluctantly, I had to let the kids go when they were about 18 months old, because I had little space in which to keep them. I was sad and sorry when that day came, but even so it was not without a touch of humour. I gave Dumpy to Alfred, a young school-leaver, who had been working for me for a short time. Alfred lived about two miles away, and it was arranged that he and his brother would lead Dumpy home on a short rope when he finished work on the Saturday morning. The trio set off cheerfully enough, and we settled down to lunch. About an hour later there was a knock at the back door. It was Alfred, out of breath and almost in tears. 'She's pulling us all over the place, and she keeps trying to come back,' he said miserably. Obstinate to the last, she had hardly gone beyond the grass on the verge outside the farm gate when she dug her feet into the ground and refused to budge any further. She stayed with us for another two days until I could arrange transport to take her to Alfred's home.

We often had other animals on the smallholding, not all of them belonging to me, and sometimes more than I could manage. The whole period of our life at The Poplars was punctuated with incidents involving livestock other than our own. The most frightening was the stampede of bullocks which came charging through the boundary fence one morning when I was quietly feeding the poultry. I was startled and wondered in which direction they may be heading. Then there was the herd of cows from the field next to mine, which trampled all over the back garden, leaving it looking like a well-used football pitch.

Our children, much to their annoyance, got the blame for this last incident, until we actually spotted the culprits breaking through the hedge and charging on to the garden.

Misty, a friend's horse which I stabled for a period, also got up to a few tricks, especially when she was feeling a bit lovelorn. More than once Nancey had to chase after her along the road to bring her back, and once we found her cavorting around a field on the other side of the road with another horse; how she got there is still a mystery, but they were certainly both thoroughly enjoying themselves.

One Sunday morning Nancey could hardly believe her eyes when she saw a huge Large White sow, followed by a dozen little piglets, coming down our drive from the field and heading towards the main gate. Luckily, we diverted them before they became entangled with the traffic on the busy road; no pork steaks for dinner that day! Nor shall I ever forget the time when two of my own pigs broke out of their sty at midnight and had us both running round in our nightclothes trying to capture them, to the accompaniment of their blood-curdling squeals. Anyone in the vicinity must have thought that murder was being committed, and we had to answer some curious questions from our neighbours the following morning.

10

I did not fully appreciate the extent of the knowledge I had acquired about poultry until I was properly established on my own smallholding. Within a few months of settling in at The Poplars, some interest in my little set-up seemed to have been created. There was a number of inquiries from local backyard poultry keepers and others eager to obtain some of the stock I had produced. At the time, however, I was not keen to part with what I hoped would be my foundation stock.

It was flattering to be called to inspect other people's poultry runs and offer them what advice I could. They also asked me to help them in the culling of their flock so that unprofitable birds could be discarded. It was true that I had gained a great deal of confidence from my year at South Mimms, which enabled me to go about my business with some assurance. Those who saw me at work must have thought that I knew what I was doing, and felt that they could trust my judgement. In a very modest way I was a kind of unofficial advisor, although I knew only too well that my own knowledge of the subject was limited, especially as there were changes and developments now taking place in the industry. Long established methods of breeding and reproduction were giving way to more scientific breeding schemes from across the Atlantic. Sexing of day-old chicks became standard practice, for example; more intensive methods of housing were being tried, and these new trends would have to be borne in mind.

Now that wartime restrictions were being removed an immediate expansion of the industry was taking place, and anyone with just a small poultry farm, like myself, without the means to expand and diversify, was economically vulnerable. It would have been possible to carry on as I was, but without additional land and extra resources there was not much future in it. Thankful as I was for my original training I was keen to get all the information possible about the changes that were taking place. It would have been easy enough for someone without sight, and without normal access to new developments, to ignore what was going on, but with the possibility of fierce competition to contend with, I felt that I had to keep up with current ideas.

The government was doing its best to encourage agricultural enterprises to try to make the country as self-sufficient in food resources as possible. There was a great deal of work to be done by the industry to replenish the numbers of livestock which had been severely depleted during the war. There was no shortage of information on every aspect of agriculture. Official pamphlets could be easily obtained on all kinds of subjects and lectures and demonstrations on the latest techniques were being frequently arranged all round the country. It was a good opportunity to keep up with what was happening at minimal expense, and I took every chance I could to get to these lectures and demonstrations, often dragging some reluctant friend along with me, because the only way of getting to some of the remote venues was to be taken there.

Living near to Preston, almost in the centre of Lancashire, we were well situated for the larger agricultural events, and although I was unable to take advantage of the visual displays and exhibits connected with poultry, it was a good opportunity to meet other poultry farmers. Demonstrators and exhibitors gave me extra attention when they realised that I was unable to see. In this way I became acquainted with several of the leading breeders. In those days Lancashire was noted for having some first-class poultry breeders and at these shows I got a great deal of advice and encouragement from them. Some of them supplied me with some of my best breeding stock.

It was at my first County Agricultural Show that I began to collect my small library on poultry husbandry. I do not think Nancey realised what she was letting herself in for when I bought these books, because as they were in ordinary print and not in Braille she had to read them to me.

When the Royal Agricultural Show was held in Lancashire shortly after the war I picked up some literature about an examination on poultry husbandry under the auspices of The Poultry Association of Great Britain. The examination, on the practical and theoretical aspects of poultry husbandry, was held over two days in Leamington Spa, and the successful candidates were awarded the Certificate of Poultry Farming. Candidates were expected to know about all aspects of poultry management, including diagnosis of diseases, basic dietary requirements, accounts, and also to be able to pluck and dress poultry for the table. As I was already doing a lot of reading on the subject and also had the solid grounding from my St Dunstan's training I decided to enter for the next examination, and I sent for an application form. This was to take place in July the following year.

I was now not quite 30 years old, and apart from a basic army educational certificate I had no other qualifications. Like many others of my generation I left school at the customary age of 14. With my scant academic background some people thought I was crazy to be going in for exams, especially now that I was unable to see. They may have been right, but for me it was another challenge. As my family and acquaintances will confirm, I am not lacking in stubbornness; this was just another example of this trait. My determination to succeed always increased in proportion to the opposition.

Preparing for the exam involved Nancey in much more reading of textbooks and specimen exam papers, often late into the night when most normal people are asleep in bed. In addition I picked the brains of local experts, and got as much information as I could from anyone I thought might be able to help: breeding stations, hatcheries, poultry food manufacturers and the like. Much of what I gleaned was in excess of what was needed, but I was not going to take chances, not knowing what would be expected of me as a candidate. If I did not know as much as I thought I ought to know, I could at least look the part, so I bought a new brown overall and a new white apron to wear when I had to pluck and dress the fowl for the table. My mother came to look after the children, and the good neighbours from across the road agreed once again to look after the livestock so that Nancey could accompany me to Kenilworth, near Leamington Spa, where the examination was to take place.

This was a completely new experience for me and I can still recall the state of my nerves the night before the exam. It was the first major educational examination of my life, and there was no guarantee of my success. The hotel, which we had chosen at random from a list that was supplied to us did nothing to lessen my anxieties. The only good thing about it was that it was very close to the railway station. It was bare and austere, and the food was of a similar standard. As we were approaching it Nancey remarked that it looked a bit seedy and we considered the possibility of finding somewhere else, but unfortunately when we got near, the proprietor popped out and saw us coming with our luggage so we had no chance of escaping. The quality of the food did not matter too much to me, as I was not feeling like eating anything. I spent a sleepless night going over and over in my mind as much as I could remember of what had been read to me over the past months.

It was a very hot July day when we arrived at the farm where the exam was to be held. All the officials and examiners could not have been more helpful to me, but this did little to settle my nerves. Because of my blindness it was agreed by the examiners that I should have an extended viva voce examination in addition to the practical tests. When the time came for me to kill and pluck my table bird I was getting more relaxed, as this was a part of the test I ought to pass without difficulty. The only trouble I had was with the livestock that were crawling about the bird which I was given to pluck and dress, because there was nothing I could do to stop these lively little creatures crawling up my arms and other parts of my body. Later, whilst I was dressing the fowl I was conscious that I was attracting a lot of attention from a group of bystanders who seemed fascinated as I sharpened my boning knife and got to work disembowelling my specimen carcass.

The last memory I have of that day is waiting by the bus-stop, smiling and sighing with relief that the ordeal was over, and being offered a lift back to town by a friendly young woman in a luxurious car. The gesture took us by surprise, as I had not come across this kind of practice since the end of the war. We did not see much of Leamington itself on that occasion, but we left with a favourable impression of the town.

The sun was still shining when we arrived back in Farington, as it had been on that day four years previously when we first occupied The Poplars. I never thought then that I would have the confidence to enter an open examination in poultry husbandry. The fact that I had been able to attempt this test gave me some satisfaction, regardless of the result. I had proved to myself that I was capable of doing things in the poultry farming world just as efficiently as other people. I knew this from the fact that not all the candidates on the course had been able to manage parts of the exam paper and this was a hopeful sign for me. From my discussions with the other candidates I considered that I stood as good a chance as most of them at passing the examination. I tried to put the whole thing out of my mind, and not to dwell on the possibility of success or failure. As far as I could see, either way could not affect me very much in the daily running of my small farm. If I was successful I would have the quiet satisfaction that I had at least convinced the examiners of my proficiency.

I had not long to wait. Within less than a week I received a letter from the Headquarters of the Poultry Association of Great Britain informing me that I had passed. On the published report I was pleased to note that I had been specially commended for my handling of the table bird section. The certificates were to be presented at the National Poultry Show at Olympia, London in October.

When the time came Nancey accompanied me. For me it was a very special occasion as this was the highest examination award I had ever received. The following week, much to our surprise, a photograph of me being handed the certificate appeared in *The Bury Times*, the newspaper company where I had served my apprenticeship as a printer after leaving school. Until then I did not realise that anyone other than my immediate family was aware of my success.

Modern Poultry Keeping, the official weekly of the Poultry Association also printed the results of the examination and a piece about the event at Olympia. Shortly afterwards I was surprised to receive a letter from the proprietor of a large poultry establishment in the south of England, offering me a job as manager of a poultry farm if I was interested. No doubt it was then within my capabilities if I had been thinking along those lines, but when I requested further information and mentioned my sight problems the offer was promptly withdrawn. I took this put-down philosophically with a smile, knowing that this was not my first experience of this kind nor was it likely to be the last. It was good preparation for other similar discriminations that were to come in future years.

Two years later I had another minor success when I was one of the successful competitors in the National Laying Trials which had been taking place over the previous 12 months on the Trial Grounds in Surrey. The presentation on this occasion was made at the Russell Hotel in London and because our infant daughter, Susan, had gone down with measles, Nancey could not come with me.

I was awarded one of the many trophies for the excellent performance of one of my Rhode Island Reds in a pen of six which had produced 285 eggs over the test period of 330 days. It was one of the many cups being awarded to successful competitors in the National Laying Trials. My prizewinning hen was not the supreme champion of the trials that year, but I was pleased it was in with a chance. Two hundred and eighty-five eggs in 330 days under natural conditions was good enough for me as a beginner in this sphere. When I returned home with the cup I found Susan was much improved, and for a long time afterwards she associated the cup with her attack of measles and was convinced that I had brought it home for her.

With these small successes to my credit I was encouraged to attempt more ambitious objectives in the poultry industry. Having proved my capabilities I thought it would be not too difficult to convince others, especially anyone connected with the higher levels of training in poultry husbandry, but to make any headway was more difficult than I thought. When I made inquiries about how I could extend my skill and knowledge I came up against polite rejections once again. With further academic training and experience I believed that I could make some personal advancement and make a greater contribution to the poultry business. I first made inquiries at the Lancashire Agricultural College about studying for the National Diploma in Poultry Husbandry, but I was told that I did not have the necessary educational standard to qualify for the course. It was also pointed out that they had no experience of dealing with blind students.

I then wrote to the recently formed British Empire Society for the Blind inquiring about their overseas programme for training blind poultry keepers. It occurred to me that they may be able to use my services in training the disadvantaged blind people of the Commonwealth in the basic skill of poultry keeping. In the event, the idea was not totally rejected, but it was suggested that such a scheme was impracticable at that particular time. I now understand that a similar scheme to the one I proposed came into operation at a later date in certain underdeveloped countries.

From that point onwards I concentrated on developing my own enterprise at The Poplars, and continued to study under my own steam. I was still keen to learn all I could about poultry, pestering Nancey to read books and magazine articles, attending lectures and demonstrations, and putting into practice some of my own theories; still hoping for an opportunity to spread my wings in the kind of life I had grown to enjoy.

11

There were no material benefits from my successes, but it had done me good to take part in activities which had taken me beyond the farm-gate into wider circles of society. It was possibly from this point forward that I became more involved with organisations and groups outside my immediate family and neighbourhood. Apart from our connections with the local Methodist Church, with which we were automatically connected on our arrival in the district, our only contact with the neighbourhood had been with our good friends, the Bilsborrows, and the local traders.

There is no direct link between my poultry farming interests and my increasing involvement with the Methodist Church, apart from the timing and opportunity. Both concerns seemed to expand simultaneously, arising from my circumstances. I cannot say that I was consciously striving towards any specific purpose at the time. My main objective then, as it continued to be, was just to be accepted as a fellow-being in my own right, with something to give back to the world. There may have been a subconscious restlessness urging me on, but I was unaware of where it might be taking me. I was quite content to let things take their course and explore any likely openings for further developments as they occurred.

My relationship with the Church at the time was nominal and tenuous. I had not been actively involved in church life since my Sunday school days, although I had remained passively interested throughout my army service. My attitude was still the same after I had lost my sight. My introduction to serious theology and preaching occurred unexpectedly and almost accidentally.

The notion of me becoming a preacher may even have been planted in my childhood, a fact I could easily have forgotten about, had I not been reminded of it many times. At the early age of eight, when the living-room of our 'two up, two down' terraced house was being decorated in preparation for my father's return from hospital, I acted the part of a preacher on the decorator's step-ladder. The incident seemed to impress the decorator, but when I was asked later to repeat the performance, I stubbornly refused, and never again did I act the role of a preacher until I did it for real when I was nearly 30 years old.

The possibility of lay preaching cropped up briefly during my time in the army in India, but it never progressed further than reading the scriptures in church. This was at a time when I came under the influence of the Rev F E Poad, a Methodist chaplain, shortly after the battalion arrived in Lahore. My colleagues of those days were also encouraging and supportive, and had I remained in the same place and with the same company I might have made more progress. I was also impressed at that time by a book on public speaking by Dale Carnegie, which fired my imagination and filled me with enough confidence to believe that the terrors of public speaking could be overcome, a terror which is never completely defeated.

There was nothing further from my mind than becoming a local preacher when we began to attend the Methodist Church in Leyland a few weeks after Paul was born. In fact, I had not thought it possible to do the work of a preacher now that I was without eyesight. The church was about two miles distant from where we lived, and we were not conveniently located for getting there. Nor was it possible, at the time, for us both to attend the services together now that we had a child to look after. I could reach the church unescorted, by a quiet country route on foot, once I had memorised the various twists and turns. It was whilst I was attending a morning service that it was announced from the pulpit that one of the senior local preachers of the church was organising a short course on basic theology. This would be held at his home on Tuesday evenings. I did not then know much about the gentleman, or where he lived, but I was interested in the idea. The course was originally intended for younger men and women, and as I was getting past that age-group, and was also blind, I thought that I might be unsuitable. The classes were to be held weekly on a Tuesday evening. Even if I was allowed to participate, I did not know how to get to the leader's house my geography of Leyland was then almost non-existent.

I need not have worried about the age factor, because once the studies got under way, I was the only person to take part for the first few sessions. Nor did the fact that I could not see prove a hindrance. The mobility problem, too, was soon overcome. Two short bus journeys and a short walk through unfamiliar streets had to be negotiated but after the first two or three meetings I was able to find my own way. Prior to this I was met from the bus by Bill Swire, the local preacher concerned. Changing buses and crossing roads gave me my most anxious moments, but this little exercise helped me in getting to know more about the layout of Leyland.

Preaching as the end product was not mentioned until after the group had been meeting for several weeks. There were never more than four people in the group, and none of us had any preaching experience except Bill Swire, the leader, and Edith Bromley (Brom), Senior French Mistress at the Grammar School who joined the meeting occasionally. Then, at one of our weekly meetings Mr Swire told us that he had approached the superintendent minister of the Circuit about the possibility of forming a 'Mission Band' with our group as its nucleus. There were no youngsters amongst us. There was Walter, who was a few years older than I, and Ken and his wife, Gladys, who were a similar age to myself.

A 'Mission Band' is a dated expression to describe a small group of people who conduct services in chapels and churches, under the supervision of a leader who does not necessarily take an active part in the service. One of the group is expected to preach a brief sermon, whilst the other members read the lessons, lead the prayers and announce the hymns. Our theology class was to become a Mission Band, and after a time arrangements were made for us to take a service at a church which was then being developed on the outskirts of Preston. The church building did not yet exist, although a site had been allocated for it, and church officials appointed. Services were held in a large house adjacent to the site, which had been bought by the church as a temporary place of worship.

Two or three weeks before the appointment I was informed that I would be the one to preach the sermon. The thought filled me with foreboding and gave me a lot of anxious moments. My immediate thoughts were, 'What am I going to preach about?', 'However shall I manage the task without sight?', and 'How will they react to having a blind preacher take their service?' This was my initiation into the office of a Methodist local preacher.

To say that my first sermon was an ordeal is an understatement. When it was over it was as though a heavy load had been lifted from my shoulders as I stepped down from the podium. There were several favourable comments, but they were lost on me in the emotional fog which descended upon me. For this initial effort in the pulpit I drew on my own experience as a soldier, employing the metaphors and imagery of warfare to get my message across, as did St Paul in his letter to Timothy, '[That] you may fight the good fight' (1 Timothy 1:18). It was an apt text, and described another kind of battle that was taking place within me as I delivered my first sermon. I had thoroughly rehearsed what I intended to say. Even so this did not prevent me from making some initial gaffes. I chose not to use Braille notes, in order to avoid drawing attention to my blindness.

The system which operates in Methodism for training mature preachers involves a prescribed course of study and constant tutorial oversight. The process may begin, as it did in my case, by becoming part of a Mission Band, or a recommendation may come from an acknowledged section of the church for an individual to receive a Note to Preach from the superintendent minister of the circuit. The On Note period may last several months under the personal direction of a senior local preacher, during which time an assessment is made of the candidate's suitability.

If the candidate receives the approval of the Preachers' Meeting, he or she moves into the On Trial period of training.

The candidate continues to be supervised during the On Trial period. Text books on theology, the scriptures and the conduct of worship have to be studied, in preparation for a compulsory examination before the candidate graduates to become an accredited local preacher. Studying to become a local preacher was by no means an easy thing for me, considering my blindness, my family commitments, and my work on the farm. In addition to the study programme, all local preachers are expected to fulfil their quota of preaching appointments each quarter, and attend the essential meetings of the church concerning local preachers' affairs.

Preaching and sermon preparation, for ministers or lay people, is a time-consuming business. Ideas and thoughts for possible themes do not come spontaneously, and when they do arise, they have to be thought through and worked at, like a sculptor chiselling away at a piece of uncut stone, sometimes for days or weeks. Even then the result is not always as satisfactory as one had hoped. Sermon construction is a craft, and like all other crafts it needs to be worked at. The technique of preaching and public speaking had been of interest to me since books on the subject were first drawn to my attention during my time in India, but of course, the opportunity to apply my interest did not occur at that time.

My first services had to be prepared down to the last detail, and as I was still reluctant to use Braille in the pulpit everything had to be committed to memory: not only the hymn numbers and the order of service, but also the passages of scripture and the outline of the sermon. Hours were spent in writing out the passages from the Bible several times until I knew them by heart. Then I would write out the sermon in full and condense it to a simple note format, which I could commit to memory.

This commitment to preaching entailed Nancey's collaboration and a certain amount of sacrifice of family life. My life might have taken a different direction had I not responded to that pulpit announcement about those theological classes and been conscripted to preach the Mission Band sermon. My curiosity has led me along many unexpected paths.

Becoming a Fully Accredited Local Preacher is not a simple matter. Regular reports are made to the Preachers' Meeting, and the training period culminates in an oral examination before the trainee's fellow preachers, in the case of the examination, and a Trial Sermon preached to a representative congregation and ministerial and lay examiner. The successful candidate's name is then brought before the church authorities for approval.

Often during this On Trial period trainees receive invitations to speak to various groups within the church. Ladies' meetings and Guilds make modest demands on the 'On Trials' to fill gaps in their lists of speakers. Addressing these small groups is good experience for anyone aspiring to become a preacher. I gained considerable experience from speaking to small, intimate groups of this kind.

The status of becoming a Fully Accredited Local Preacher is marked by a Public Recognition Service. In due course I did reach this stage, but not without a lot of physical and mental energy on my part, and much patience on the part of those who were responsible for the completion of my training. One person who believed that I would make the grade was the man who 'commanded' that I preach the sermon at our first Mission Band service, but, sadly, he did not live to see it. He died the very night I reached the second stage of my training. It looked as though I was taking up the work as he was laying it down.

My own Recognition Service took place in Leyland, and was probably the most significant event in my life so far, even more important to me than the passing of poultry exams and gaining accolades for prizewinning hens. It was also a special event, for other reasons: three of us, Colin, Walter, and myself, became local preachers at the same recognition service, which was a rare occurrence in the life of Methodism. The ceremony does not confer any special privileges other than the authority to conduct services in Methodist churches but it was good to feel that we had the support of congregations from many quarters. I was particularly moved to know that there were many people present from Bolton Road Methodist Church in Bury, which I had attended in my younger days. The Sunday school teachers may have despaired at times in their efforts to inculcate Christian values into a class of junior schoolboys, especially when parodied versions of hymns came from the squeaky, treble voices of lads in short trousers. I cannot sing the last verse of 'What a Friend we have in Jesus' today, without recalling those carefree days when we sang in chorus, 'Thou shalt find a shoelace there', instead of 'Thou shalt find a solace there.' Those long-suffering teachers must share some of the credit for planting the seeds of Christian understanding in my mind.

My first opportunity to speak to a large outdoor audience arose when the Bolton Road church invited me to open the Memorial Hall, an extension to the church premises which had been built to commemorate former Sunday school scholars who had died in the two world wars. My brief speech, which took weeks of anxious preparation and which was delivered with equally torturous anxiety, appeared to be well received, and even attracted the notice of some of my ex-colleagues on *The Bury Times*. It appeared in print a few days later, much to my surprise. For my pains I was presented with a ceremonial key, and given the Freedom of the Memorial Hall. For a brief moment as I raised my voice I was back on the parade ground and I then felt much more at home. It was also a group of ladies from the church in Bury who first invited me to talk about my own experiences as a blind person, and to tell the St Dunstan's story as I knew it. Initially, it was a daunting prospect which forced me to examine the course of my life since I was wounded close to the banks of the Irrawaddy several years previously.

Shortly after I had become a local preacher I realised one of my secret ambitions. This was to preach from the plainly-carved pale pulpit below which I had once wriggled and squirmed as a youngster listening to the sonorous tones of those who were in their day regarded as the 'pulpit giants' of Methodism. Appropriately and symbolically it was the Harvest Festival services at which I was asked to preach, and it could not have been a more fulfilling homecoming for me. I was greeted by the voices of family and friends, many of whom I could still recognise in spite of the passing of time and of now being unable to see them. After the morning service, a man greeted me with, 'You won't remember me', he said, I'm Geoffrey Smith!' I had not seen Geoffrey since we were close neighbours as schoolboys and since then he had moved to the south of England. He was surprised when I told him that I remembered him well and that his birthday was on 24th August. Geoff and I had been playmates since we were toddlers so it was not surprising that I remembered a lot about him. We had grown up together until our lives had taken different courses in our adolescent years.

This day of exhilaration and excitement, however, was tinged with poignancy and sadness. Two of the saddest people present at the service must have been the parents of Ernest Davis, who had been a close friend in my teenage years. Ernest was killed in action during the war when the allied armies were advancing in Italy. I wrote to him last from India, but the letter was returned to me a few weeks later conveying this sad fact.

The convergence of these personal associations and emotions, bringing past and present experiences together on such an occasion confirmed the direction that my life was to take from that point forward. There was no remuneration or any expectations of social advantage from becoming a local preacher, but I felt that it was the right thing to do. In retrospect, it has been the gateway into a fuller and richer life than I could possibly have dreamed of when I was first presented with the challenge to begin my studies.

12

As a fully commissioned local preacher, I accepted that much would be expected of me, and that there would be increased pressures on my time and energy. First of all, I was expected to be theologically literate, and I realised that from now on I had much to learn if I was to prove myself adequate to the task. I would also need to keep up with current theological thinking, and to be conversant with local and national events in the Church, and in the world.

The main problems to overcome were sermon preparation and mobility. During my On Trial period I could rely on the guidance of those who trained me as far as my sermons were concerned; and on my good friend Bill Johnson, in his two-ton Bedford lorry, for most of my transport needs. Once I was on my own, however, I had to give some thought to the practical implications of doing these things independently when necessary.

Sermon preparation, properly done, involves time, effort, and access to a wide range of theological sources, as well as an awareness of contemporary issues. It was not as though most things were not available to me in one form or another: Braille, talking book or tape, or, quite often, Nancey reading to me from my own stock of books. Whichever means I used had its limitations. The chief enemy was time – the amount of hours available to me for research was limited – and the task of setting it down for intelligible presentation was also time-consuming.

No sooner had one service been completed than the next appointment in the pulpit was looming. Seldom is any preacher, minister or layperson like myself, technically satisfied with his performance in the pulpit, in spite of the plaudits offered by an appreciative congregation. Preaching for me has always meant the striving for perfection in the execution of a sermon, from the inception of an idea to its final utterance. By experience one learns to adjust one's approach, and achieve a proper balance.

Preparation of a service or sermon varies with the occasion and with the individual preacher. My preferred method is one which I picked up from a book on the subject many years ago. It was suggested that materials and ideas for different subjects and Bible texts be placed in separately-labelled envelopes as they occur to you. When a particular theme for a sermon is required, materials to support it can be easily found, and arranged to form the basis of the sermon or talk.

Since I have been preaching I have tried to avoid using pulpit notes. Braille notes can be difficult to handle without distracting the congregation. In the early stages I typed my sermons in full, under distinct headings. The typescript was no use to me as such, but the fact that I had written it out helped to imprint my thoughts more firmly in memory. Every service I conduct becomes a memory test. Not only has the outline of the sermon to be remembered, but also the order of service, passages of scripture, hymn numbers and church announcements.

From the time I realised that my blindness was permanent I knew that I would always have to be more dependent on my memory than I had been previously. This had not been so important to me before, but now I had to try to cultivate my memory, if only to prove to other people that I could cope with any situation in the pulpit. It was not always easy to convince the vestry officials of this, especially when I did not carry any books or aids into the pulpit with me. I confidently assured everyone concerned that all that was needed was for someone to lead me to the pulpit steps, and from then on everything would be all right. After some time I was credited with the title of the Memory Man but, of course, this was an exaggeration.

Getting to churches had to be planned well in advance, but this did not always prevent some minor embarrassments and confusion once I had arrived. Trying to find my way around the church furniture before the service began could be awkward, until the vestry stewards realised that I was unable to see. In unfamiliar pulpits it is often a matter of guesswork locating the direction and the size of the congregation, until I get some idea during the singing of the hymns.

Bill Johnson, my greengrocer friend, had volunteered his services as my chauffeur as soon as I took up this work, and willingly took me to most of my appointments throughout my period of training. The local congregations had got used to me arriving at the door of their churches in a greengrocer's lorry, but I could not expect him to carry on doing this indefinitely, now that I would have to take more appointments each quarter. Without his assistance I would have had to restrict my preaching to churches which were easily reached. Once I was familiar with the area I had less difficulty in getting to my appointments under my own steam – by 'shanks's pony', bus and on occasion, by train.

There are many anecdotes about local preachers who have had to walk many miles in all kinds of weather to preach to small isolated congregations, so when my turn came I was not expecting any special consideration. In fact I quite enjoyed the challenge of getting to places on my own, although there would have been no lack of willing helpers if needed.

But getting to an appointment could also take up a lot of time. One took me five and a half hours from leaving home and returning – four bus journeys, two half-hour walks, and a one-hour church service. These trips were negotiated without any serious mishap, but there were occasions when things did not go according to plan, like the time when I arrived at a church hot, breathless and ten minutes late. The church was about three miles from home; I felt sure that I knew the way, and did not seek any help until it was too late. I had somehow missed a turning in the road, which completely disorientated me. All the officials of the church had gone looking for me, and were relieved when they spotted my white stick moving along the edge of the pavement as I scurried along.

There have been anxious moments in travelling to appointments, especially if I was going to a place for the first time. It has been known for me to arrive for a service looking a bit dishevelled from an encounter with an unsuspected obstacle. Even if I had carefully planned my journey beforehand things could often go awry. It was always a help if I could be met from the bus or train by someone from the church I was visiting. I have come a cropper several times, even in the shortest distance from bus to church gates, when I have attempted it on my own. Low garden walls, rain-soaked hedges, telegraph poles and badly placed trees were amongst the worst hazards, to say nothing of cycles and other objects strewn unthinkingly on the ground. Bumps on my forehead, caused by colliding with some obstacle, have invited some curious comments when I have had to explain what happened. Solid walls are not so bad to cope with if they are high enough not to fall over, but hedges are a menace for blind people travelling alone, especially when there are overhanging branches, and doubly so when it has been raining.

Preaching has given me many experiences and opportunities that no one would have thought possible had they seen me that day in January 1945 as I lay at death's door on the battlefield. There have been impressive and moving occasions, as well as many humorous and embarrassing ones. Once I was invited to preach in a church in Bolton where a young married couple with two small children were my hosts for the day. I had written to them to explain about my blindness, and to assure them that I would be able to cope with any domestic arrangements. I usually did this to save any embarrassment – on both sides – when we met. After lunch it was arranged that I should take it easy, whilst the parents took the youngsters for a walk in the countryside. No sooner had they set off than the children were back home without their parents. They were more interested in this strange person who could not see, rather than doing something that they could do any other day. They had given their mum and dad the slip and had come back to bombard me with questions: 'Was I a goodie or a baddie?';

'Was I a cowboy or an Indian?'; 'Was I 'deaded' in the war?', and many more such interrogations. For an hour or more I was grilled about my becoming blind! When the parents returned ready to tell them off, their annoyance turned to amusement to discover us engaged in a serious discussion about war blindness. Another amusing incident occurred following my visit to a local Sunday school. One little boy went home proudly announcing that 'blind Jesus' had been to their Sunday school that day.

One of the funniest incidents occurred on the landing stage at Bowness on Lake Windermere. Nancey and I had just come off one of the pleasure steamers and Nancey had gone to the Ladies Room whilst I went to the Gents. As I was returning she met me; she had discovered that she had not got the necessary penny and was just asking me if I had one, when a voice right at my elbow said, 'Here's a penny, Mrs Taylor. I have heard Mr Taylor preach many times, and it's always worth a penny to hear him!' I did not recognise the voice, but obviously the person had remembered me. Local preaching is an unpaid service, which gives rise to the old joke that local preachers are 'good for nothing' – this was one time when I was good for a penny.

One of the most rewarding experiences I associate with preaching occurred whilst I was a representative to the annual Aggregate Meeting of the Local Preachers Mutual Aid Association which looks after the needs of local preachers and their dependants. The gathering took place in London and I was invited to preach in two Methodist churches in Bromley in Kent. Mr and Mrs Anderson, with whom I stayed for the weekend, had a young Muslim student in their home as a paying guest. He was studying pharmacology at one of the London colleges, and in the course of conversation we discovered some common interests, and also that we were both familiar with Lahore in the Punjab in North India and Durban in South Africa.

Those points of contact helped us to establish a relationship in spite of our different religious backgrounds, he a devout Muslim and myself a practising

Christian. On the Sunday afternoon we took a stroll in the nearby park, in the spring weather of early June, and we shared our experiences and beliefs as we went along. When we returned to the house I was delighted when I learned that he had asked Mrs Anderson if she thought I would mind if he attended the evening service to hear me preach. Of course there was no objection on my part, and he paid me the compliment of coming along with me. What effect my preaching had on him I may never know, but I like to think that it was a successful piece of missionary work.

It is always a pleasure to be invited to preach in the St Dunstan's chapel in Ovingdean at the annual Memorial Service, which commemorates the death of Sir Arthur Pearson, the founder of St Dunstan's. Sir Arthur was President of the National Institute for the Blind when St Dunstan's was founded in 1915. He lost his sight due to glaucoma but in spite of this he had a good reputation as a journalist, and was an eminent newspaper and magazine owner – he founded the *Daily Express*. He died on the 9th December 1921. The Memorial Service is a timely reminder of the origins and purposes of the organisation, and an opportunity to remember the debt owed to this man of vision and enterprise. I was privileged to give the address on one of these special occasions, when I spoke about the invaluable inheritance handed down from our predecessors. The lesson was read by Sir Neville Pearson, the son of Sir Arthur.

Over the years I have been asked to preach in many different parts of the country, from Cumbria to Cornwall, and from Liverpool to Norfolk. Wherever my preaching has taken me, to small country chapels or large down-town churches, I have been conscious of following in the footsteps of eminent preachers and it is a humbling experience. This was how I felt when I was invited to preach in the church in Bolton Road in Bury, the church where I had been nurtured in the faith. It was here that I had been captivated by the thunderous voices and charisma of the outstanding preachers of my childhood, the models I had tried to imitate in the kitchen of our terraced house. Many years had elapsed since I had sat on the front pew and looked up in awe at many of these characters, reminiscent of the Old Testament prophets, never thinking that one day I would stand where they were standing.

I had similar feelings the first time I preached in Lancaster, in the church I attended as a young soldier when I sat in the back pew and listened to a Rev Smith preach a sermon on giving. I can still hear him bellowing with frightening authority, 'Shrouds have no pockets.' Nothing could have been further from my mind, dressed as I was in my khaki uniform, that one day I would stand in that very same pulpit.

An awesome presence seems to linger about many of the older pulpits where I know that some of the household names of Methodism have preached. There is still a 'Wesley' pulpit in a nearby circuit which, I am sure, is impregnated with the aura of the great man himself.

Local preachers in training are supervised by senior preachers. To be asked to perform this for a new preacher is an honour, and doubly so if one is invited to share in their Recognition Service. It has been my pleasure to have been involved in the training and management of several candidates, including that of my son, Paul, who is now a Methodist minister, and to have delivered the 'charge' to preach to four of my erstwhile colleagues, two of whom have also been ordained in the Methodist Church.

13

For several months before my Recognition Service my preaching future had been in doubt because of my health, which consequently led to a change of occupation, change of address, and eventually to a change in academic standing. Both my farming and preaching activities were interrupted for a time following surgery for a duodenal ulcer.

I took up the work again as soon as possible, but not without first hearing some discouraging noises from family and friends, who thought that I ought to give up preaching altogether. I was also advised to curtail my work on the farm. Preaching was the most demanding thing I had done for some time, and no doubt it had affected my health. However, in spite of the pain and discomfort, I felt a sense of purpose and achievement in what I was doing, and I was determined not to quit.

I was faced with a dilemma. I got a lot of satisfaction from poultry farming, and although I was still keen to continue, there was no way of extending my interest in this field with insufficient remuneration from my reduced physical resources. Not being able fully to occupy myself and pay my way properly on the farm, I became restless and dissatisfied. I cast around for another occupation, but my uncertain health and my limited educational attainments restricted my choice.

If I was going to do anything at all, a few obstacles would have to be overcome, and obstacles they were indeed; first, my lack of paper qualifications, and secondly, my ties with my smallholding. The openings for change, however, were not propitious. Getting into established education as a blind adult at the age of 34 proved more difficult than getting access to Buckingham Palace. There were plenty of courses for sighted students, but very little, if any, for mature students with sight problems.

There were day and night-school classes at very low charges in a variety of subjects, both academic and vocational, for sighted people, but nothing at all for those who could not see. It was suggested that if I wanted to do some further study the best approach might be through the County Education Authority at County Hall in Preston. I did so, and came away disappointed, without hope of making any advance in my education. The attention I received was abysmal. In effect, I was told, 'Go home and forget about it.' This was not the first time my request for assistance had been met with a patronising rebuff. It was made clear that there was no way I could be helped to get any A levels at my age and with my disability. I had been anticipating some constructive sympathy, similar to the help and encouragement which I had received shortly after returning from the Far East, although I was then several years younger.

I next approached the principal of the Harris College in Preston, then one of the largest teaching establishments in Lancashire, about the possibility of studying at the College as a blind student. The response was equally as dismissive as that from County Hall – they had no facilities for teaching blind students. He suggested that one of the Correspondence Courses might serve my purpose, but that was all the help he could offer me. As a last resort I enrolled with one of the Correspondence Courses in London, but this, too, did not prove very satisfactory. Everything came in ordinary printed form, which meant that most of the available time for studying was taken up in Nancey reading everything out to me, and this on top of her other family duties. The work itself was not too difficult, as some of my early results showed, but there was too much hassle and upheaval of the domestic routine for me to continue. Trying to become a student after a lapse of some 20 years, and now with some additional handicaps, was proving too much.

Morning after morning I sat at the dining-room table surrounded by books, typewriter and tape-recorder, listening to Nancey going over the correspondence material for me. At the rate I was going I could not see myself making much headway, so I thought it better to quit then, before I had got in too deep, and whilst the household had not been too badly disruptured. Had there been someone local who I could contact, it may have been different. After a while I gave up the idea of making any academic progress by this means, more from frustration than anything else.

My frustration was compounded by the feeling that I had something to offer, and that I was capable of using my time and experience more productively, but doing what? And where? My limited options were the stumbling block. My work as a local preacher had demonstrated my ability to cope with everything expected of someone in that position, so a vocation in that direction was a possibility. I had thought once or twice about becoming Methodist minister, but had dismissed the idea without giving it serious consideration. I was also active in local church affairs, so much so that most people became oblivious to my blindness. Why, then, I kept asking myself, was I finding it so difficult to find an outlet for the drives I knew I had? I was eager to prove to myself, if not to others, that I was able to do more with my life than I was doing at present.

I thought that the little I could offer might be of use in a voluntary capacity to some organisation on a more or less full-time basis, possibly as a local organiser or speaker. As I had been interested in the Bible Society since my introduction to it during my service days in India, and had been a member of the local group for many years, I thought that they might welcome some voluntary help; but not so. The response to my letter was brief, courteous but condescending, suggesting that other organisations may want to use my services.

A possible break came when I was attending a conference for blind farmers in Selby, Yorkshire, sponsored jointly by the North Regional Association for the Blind and a national animal feed manufacturer. The conference was interesting and instructive, and the most valuable element was my meeting up with Eric Toole, the secretary for the

110

North Region. Whilst he was driving me to the bus station for my return journey to Leyland, the conversation got round to the Home Teachers of the Blind course. He promised to send me a syllabus and an application form for the next examination, which was to take place the following July at the headquarters of the Association in Leeds. The next course began in the autumn.

The examination included written essay questions, and a rigorous interview with a selection board. All candidates were expected to have five GCE O Level passes. The one-year course covered tuition in writing and reading Braille, social welfare and administration, handicrafts, and a few other subjects relating to work among blind people. Apart from my lack of educational qualifications, I thought that I stood a good chance of being accepted. I considered myself proficient at Braille and typing, and also at certain kinds of handicrafts. My experience as a pastoral visitor and councillor might also be a point in my favour. There was nothing much that I could do about improving my educational credentials, but I thought nothing would be lost in going ahead with my application. I spent the next few months preparing myself for the entrance examination. I received marvellous support and encouragement from the local blind welfare organisation, especially from Miss Varley, my personal home teacher, who had often invited me to help her on a few of her visits, in a pastoral role. I had no difficulty in obtaining suitable references. Miss Varley helped me to learn new handicrafts and Nancey was again involved in plenty of reading. Home teaching was something I thought was within my capabilities, and I submitted my application in good time. Shortly afterwards I was notified to present myself at Headingly Castle for the entrance examination for the course.

I was no stranger to the part of Leeds where the test was to take place, but it was strange to return there after many years. I had been stationed in that area when I was in the army shortly after the outbreak of the war. As a young soldier I had been part of an advance party to staff the Teacher Training College at Becketts Park when it was requisitioned by the army for the training of medical personnel.

The hotel where Nancey and I stayed was very close to where I had once paraded in my khaki uniform. In those days the clanging of the city's trams was the loudest sound to be heard, as they drew away from the terminus at Headingly. Now there were no trams; the noises which filled the air were those of a busy shopping precinct. New shopping and residential areas had replaced the green fields, and new road systems made it hard to locate the old landmarks. There was, however, no mistaking the training college, now restored to its original function, where hundreds of wartime conscripts had been trained as army doctors, medical orderlies and nurses. I would like to have had a proper look round, but this was not possible. Nancey described the scene before me as I stood beside the iron railings of the college trying to recall the names of the student accommodation blocks; only two of the four came to mind – Fairfax and Cavendish. In my mind's eye I saw again the faces of my young barrack room-mates.

Headingly Castle was only a short walk from the hotel. As we approached it I was still thinking about the last time I was in these parts. Then, I was a young active lad in uniform with few cares and responsibilities, and with all my physical faculties. Now, I was physically limited, and dependent on others to meet most of my everyday needs. I began to think about the circumstances which had brought me to this particular turning point in my life. In my search for job satisfaction since losing my sight, I had followed several illusive paths and built up false hopes. If I was successful in this test, it would mean another change for me and my family. We were likely to be stepping out in a new direction.

When I came face to face with some of the other candidates in the waiting room I began to have some doubts about my prospects of success. They were probably all much younger than I was and already had the required educational background. I was the only one without sight though several had partial vision. They had sufficient sight for them to be able to write in manuscript, and so were able to meet as a group in one room with an invigilator. I was segregated from the others because I had opted to use my typewriter, (which I later thought was a mistake), out of three options available to me: Braille, typing and the use of an amanuensis. I was taken into a small room to work by myself without even an invigilator present for most of the time. Once the question had been read to me I was left to my own devices. It really was a horrible situation to be in. I could have done with someone there, if only to read back what I had written, and to help me relocate my position on the page when necessary. It was one of the most miserable days of my life, and my normally buoyant confidence was at a low ebb. Under the strain of the exam I was bound to make more typing errors than usual, which I had difficulty in correcting, and in addition I had to concentrate on the content of the question and remember exactly where I was in the construction of a sentence or paragraph.

I began to flag long before the time limit had been reached, and I saw my chances slipping away as the minutes passed. When the time was up my paper was collected and I was dismissed without a word being read back to me. I was sure that the result would hardly make sense in view of the haphazard way I had to tackle my corrections and alterations.

My interview with the examining board was equally disastrous. A deathly silence hit me as I entered the interview room. I was taken to a seat across the table from the presiding member of the interview board, who struck me immediately as an overbearing, late middle-aged spinster. On either side of her were the rest of my examiners, and Eric Toole, the secretary. It seemed to me that there were twice as many people on the examining board than there were candidates.

From the beginning I sensed an air of antagonism. There were no pleasantries; I was alone on my side of the long table, and from the tone and content of the interview I felt that I was being questioned for a post with MI5, rather than as a prospective student for training for work with the blind. There was no mention of my examination paper, but from the oblique references it became apparent that I was considered unsuitable material for the course. Many of the questions were so trivial, irrelevant and patronising that I became more than a little irritated – to put it mildly – which could not have improved my chances. I became even more cross when I was questioned about my general mobility capabilities. I had assured them that I was already engaged in voluntary work which involved me getting around my own locality without difficulty. I said, 'The question of my mobility would be more pertinent after my training when I was applying for jobs, rather than when I was only seeking admission for training.' This burst of aggression probably sealed my fate as far as the course was concerned! But by this time I could hardly have cared less. I breathed a great sigh of relief at the end of the interview, and no doubt this feeling was shared by everyone. As I left the room I was told that I would be informed by letter about my application.

Whilst I had been facing the ordeal of the examination, and being grilled by my interrogators, Nancey had been exploring Headingly and its shops. She was back in time to meet me out and automatically assumed my success when I greeted her with a broad smile. She made no comment when I told her that my smile did not indicate success, but a triumphant escape. I was completely turned off the idea of becoming a home teacher by what I had just experienced, but I had lost nothing by taking part in this selection process. I still continued with my voluntary teaching of Braille and typing, which I had been doing for some time already.

We took another look at Becketts Park on our way to the hotel to collect our belongings. Whatever the future might hold, it was almost certain that I would not be returning to this part of Leeds again. I don't know what was going on in Nancey's mind, but I was still reflecting upon what had brought me back to this spot after so many years. This incident would soon merge into my history of attempts to justify my existence. We collected our travelling bags from the hotel, and made for the railway station for our return journey home to await developments. No doubt Nancey was thankful that I would not be leaving her to cope alone with the home and the farm.

Within a day or so the expected letter arrived from Headingly, confirming what I had already suspected: I was not to be admitted as a student for the Home Teacher of the Blind Course in the autumn. The letter included some sugary platitudes, but as I had already decided not to pursue the idea any further, I wasn't greatly disappointed.

14

Now that my future was decided regarding the training course, I was free to continue with the teaching of Braille and typing on a voluntary basis, as I had been doing for some time. I was not overwhelmed with requests for my services, but it gave me satisfaction to know that I was capable of doing some of the work of a professional home teacher, albeit on a smaller scale. I was always ready to help whenever I was asked, because I remembered how much I appreciated the help I had received when I first lost my sight.

I was involved in teaching Braille and typing to two other blind men of my own generation: John and Gilbert. I was introduced to John by a local school master, a member of the local parish church who had been to visit John, and who was troubled by his state of health. His sight had suddenly failed as a result of the malfunctioning of his pituitary gland, which he attributed to his war service in Egypt. As a result of his condition several of his physical features had become enlarged and distorted; his hands and his chin were much larger than normal, and he had become very self-conscious about what had happened to him. According to my contact, he was in a distressed state of mind, spending most of his time withdrawn in his bedroom, or lounging about the house. When I called at his home it was pitiful to see a man, who had recently been so active, rapidly vegetating with little desire to live.

It was strange that I should be coming to John's help now, because he had once helped me without me knowing it, something he told me shortly after we met. Apparently, before he had lost his sight, he had helped me across a very busy junction when I had been standing at the roadside waiting to cross. He had been driving along, had seen my predicament, and had got out of his car to assist me. John was an engineering draughtsman with Leyland Motors, but had had to retire prematurely on health grounds. He had remained a bachelor, and lived with his sister and her husband only a mile or so along the road where I lived, but he was unknown to me until I was asked to help him.

Up to now he had not ventured out of the house alone. He was very gloomy about not being able to do anything for himself now that he was without sight, and very sceptical about his future. The first thing I did was to suggest that he should come along to see me at home under his own steam. I realised that this was asking a lot from someone newly-blind, but I was confident that if this initial obstacle could be overcome, it would be a tremendous boost to his self-confidence. Physical independence is a priceless commodity, not always appreciated by those who have it – the loss of it damages not only self-confidence, but also a large measure of self-respect. These can be gradually restored by some personal effort.

It was only a short direct bus journey between our two houses, with convenient adjacent bus stops. If someone could help John to board the bus, I would be there to meet him as he arrived. In spite of his initial doubts, and with a bit of encouragement from his family, I was delighted when John made the effort.

I had converted one of the brick outbuildings on the smallholding into a room for study purposes, where I could keep my bulky Braille books and other special equipment. It was here that John and I began to talk about him learning Braille and basic touch-typing. We discovered immediately that he would have difficulty in using Braille, because his medical problem made his fingers less sensitive, but after a short demonstration of touch-typing on my small portable machine, he became quite enthusiastic about getting started on learning the keyboard. For the next couple of months John came several times a week until he had learned to type accurately without difficulty. During this short time his attitude towards life was transformed and he gained enough confidence to walk unaided to and from his home when the weather permitted. He was obviously enjoying his new-found freedom. Now that his prospects had brightened he applied to attend the rehabilitation centre in Torquay, and to his great satisfaction was invited for rehabilitation and employability assessment. Following this, and backed up with his newly-acquired basic typing skill, he was accepted for training and given a more professional course in audio typing. At the completion of the course he rejoined the payroll at Leyland Motors as an audio typist, doing internal memos. There was joy and pleasure among his family, friends and old colleagues when he regained full-time work with his former employers. Sadly, his health deteriorated due to his glandular disorder, and he died after a few years back at work. I like to think that, although he may not have had a long life, he had the satisfaction that, during his last years, he was some use to himself and to other people.

I first met Gilbert when I was visiting St Dunstan's training and rehabilitation centre at Ovingdean, Brighton in 1963. Our meeting was literally accidental: I had just entered the lounge, and was trying to locate a vacant seat, when I collided with Gilbert in his wheelchair. As we readjusted ourselves and settled down to chat we discovered that we had things in common. From then onwards the friendship grew. Like John, Gilbert's sight did not fail until several years after the war, and this was his first visit to the centre at Ovingdean. Gilbert had only recently become a member of St Dunstan's. His blindness was attributed to his war service with the RAF in Malta and he also suffered from the crippling rheumatic condition, anchylising spondylitis. He had come through the wartime siege of Malta unscathed; now, not only had he lost his sight, he was also crippled, spending most of his waking hours in his wheelchair. His illness caused him to be so bent over, that, instead of standing six feet tall, his normal height, he was now less than five feet.

In spite of the constant pain and discomfort Gilbert was determined to get everything he could out of life. Under normal circumstances he would have had the benefit of concentrated training and expert tuition at St Dunstan's, to enable him to enjoy as full and active a life as possible.

Unfortunately, because of his frequent spells in hospital, it was not possible for him to do the standard training course.

When the welfare department of St Dunstan's knew that I was willing to assist Gilbert they supported the idea of some home tuition. The arrangement was that I should visit him for a couple of hours each Tuesday. Nancey took me to Preston in our car, and I made my own way to Silverdale by train, where I would be met by and taken to their home. After the session I was taken back to the railway station where I could catch my train to Preston.

On my arrival Gilbert's wife, Margaret, prepared a snack before leaving for her work as a private secretary. Then it really was a case of 'the blind leading the blind', but apart from the occasional spillage on the kitchen worktop, we did not create any problems. Should anything have gone disastrously wrong neighbours were not far away, but thankfully we never had to call on them. Margaret had left everything ready for a final cup of tea before I left.

I was conscious that Gilbert was in constant pain from his spondylitis, though he seldom mentioned it. It must have taken tremendous guts to concentrate on making sense of the elusive braille dots, and coping with the complexities of a typewriter keyboard while in pain, and also without sight. It was amazing how quickly he grasped the principle of the Braille system, although we made only slow progress in actual reading. When it came to typing, the many laughs over the inevitable humorous incidents must have had some therapeutic value – two blind men fumbling with an awkward typewriter, when neither of us could see what was happening. The social value of the visit, I believe, was as important as the educational aspect and the experience of introducing the intricacies of Braille and touch-typing to another person was a help to me as well as to Gilbert.

Gilbert collapsed and died whilst I was with him on one of my weekly visits. He was by then only a shadow of a man, battling to the end, and still eager to learn and make the most of life. There was nothing more now that I could do for Gilbert, nor could I give much practical help to Margaret in the crisis. However, thanks to the training I had received, and my experience of blindness since the tragic death of my grandmother which had occurred when I was newly-blind, I now felt better equipped to cope with the situation, and was able to bring a measure of comfort and consolation to Margaret and her family.

John and Gilbert could so easily have given up, but such was their spirit that, given an opportunity, they were ready to make full use of it. The fact that it was I who happened to be present at the time of need was only coincidental. Whether or not I could have been of more use to John and Gilbert had I been professionally trained it is hard to say; I was only passing on some of the skills which had been given to me.

15

Whilst I was still visiting Gilbert in Silverdale, and meeting John each week, I was also still preaching and involved in pastoral work. Then two unsolicited opportunities for public service came my way almost simultaneously; both were voluntary jobs in wider public service. I welcomed these propositions as an indication that I still had something to offer to the world – my self-confidence was restored after the previous rebuttals.

The first one was to become a worker with the Probation Service, as a prison visitor and aftercare supporter. The second was an invitation to become a member of the advisory council for BBC Radio Blackburn, the proposed new local radio station to be set up in Lancashire. These came at a time when opportunities for higher education were being presented by the newly-constituted Open University, then preparing to open its doors to such people as myself. This news was just what I had been waiting for. At the age of 45 it seemed as though my life was about to take off in various new and unexplored directions.

These were not the only changes that were to affect Nancey and me in the near and also the more distant future. Within the next 12 months we had left the smallholding and were adjusting to a new daily routine, in a new home, in unfamiliar surroundings. The children had now left home – Susan had married Stephen earlier in the year, and Paul was working in Derbyshire as a lay pastor before going to college. Moving into a different house in a different locality along with the other imminent changes may have been traumatic, but they were also a spur and challenge to me personally.

My friend Harry, a local preacher and probation officer, introduced me to the voluntary section of the Probation Service. It arose out of a series of special services we did together with local church congregations on Social

Responsibility, and Penal Reform. At the conclusion of the series Harry invited me to meet his immediate superior, with a view to becoming a volunteer with the Probation Service. I had little knowledge about the workings of the law and the prison system. The extent of my dealings with anyone in custody up to now had been restricted to escorting military prisoners whilst I was in the army. The thought of getting involved in this work had not occurred to me until Harry mentioned it. Before I was accepted as a volunteer I went through the usual vetting process and had a short training course. The work consisted mainly of establishing relationships with, and generally befriending, offenders and ex-offenders on a one-to-one basis.

This type of prison visiting was done by mutual agreement between the volunteer and the inmate. The visits were in addition to the normal visiting regulations, each prisoner having the option whether or not to make use of the scheme. Of course, this could not be done without the co-operation of the prison authorities.

My first assignment was with Jim, who was then coming towards the end of his sentence in Preston prison. Jim had spent a lot of time in prison and was getting to an age when, if he did not make a break soon, reoffending and spells in prison could be the pattern for the rest of his life. Before I could visit him I had to write to ask him to get things moving and send me a Visiting Order. Establishing a relationship at a distance in these circumstances was not the easiest thing to do and in my first letter I could only introduce myself and give a few details about my background and interests. I mentioned my blindness, but I did not want to put him off by making too much of it. I wondered how he might react, but as things turned out he accepted me without questioning either my blindness or the sincerity of my motives.

This was my first visit to prison. On my journey there, by bus, I had some misgivings, and wondered how I would be received, not only by Jim, but also by the officers. It was recognised that prison visitors were tolerated rather than welcomed by some members of the prison staff, who were inclined to regard people doing this work as the 'do gooding brigade'. Usually when I am travelling alone I am too busy concentrating on the hazards I am likely to meet, but this time my thoughts were fixed on how I would cope with this new experience, and the new relationship I was about to enter into.

A passer-by helped me locate the doorbell when he noticed me hesitating in the gateway of the prison. Once inside I was led into a small waiting-room whilst telephone messages went round the prison to find Jim. The first thing that struck me as I sat waiting to be escorted across the prison yard to the main visitors' room was the heat from the radiator at my side. True enough, it was a bright, chilly, autumn afternoon, but I was not expecting prison to be quite so warm.

A prison officer led me to a table and it was a few more minutes before Jim arrived, escorted by another prison officer. I stood up and held out my hand as a friendly gesture, which seemed to take him by surprise. The prison officer, too, seemed taken aback by this move. Then it was my turn to be surprised for no sooner had we taken our seats at a small table, than we were brought cups of tea.

Conversation was awkward and stilted until we got to know each other a bit better, and were able to discover some common areas of interest. Jim was ready to talk about his younger life in Glasgow as a choirboy and server in the church, and his later life as a seaman in the merchant navy. He had been to many of the places I had visited in my army travels. He was well-read, and had interesting stories to tell. Right from the start there was nothing morbid or mawkish about our discussion, in fact they were interspersed with much laughter and amusement.

Until then, like most people, I had a stereotyped image of prisons and their occupants. I had still to learn that the majority of inmates are ordinary people like myself, and that prisons are microcosms of society, holding a complex range of personality types, not just one special category on whom we stick the label 'prisoner'.

In a face-to-face situation Jim's personality was warm and affable, although he did admit that part of his problem was the bottle. He confessed that the worst part of life inside prison was not the severity of the conditions, but the deprivation of liberty, the humiliation and degradation. Many visits later he told me how important that initial visit had been and what impression it had made on him. Jim had taken in everything about my appearance. He particularly liked the green shirt I had been wearing, and asked where he might get a similar one. On subsequent visits he mentioned this, and told me he was making extra efforts to arrive smartly dressed for our meetings.

I met Jim on the morning of his discharge, over a mug of tea in the bus station café, when he began to make the mental adjustment to life outside prison, and to orientate himself for the future. Before we separated, he said that he would like to come to church with me on the following Sunday. We arranged to meet, but he did not turn up; the thought of coming face to face with the public in such a context was possibly too much for him. After this, contact was lost until I got a letter from him in which told me that he was about to get married to a young local woman. After a while I had another letter to tell me that his wife was expecting a baby. In other letters he reflected, sometimes in verse, on the futility of prison life. Although I have now lost touch with Jim, I often think about him, and hope that his life is now more settled and happy.

The volunteers met together as a group about every two months, to report, to share our experiences, and to learn more about this type of social work. We were a mixed bunch, representing a cross-section of the community: men, women, young and old, not all of them churchgoers. There were tradesmen and shop assistants, as well as a few from the professions; occasionally we had an ex-offender in the group. There was plenty of scope, in a group of this kind, to handle many of the problems facing discharged offenders. Employment and housing accommodation were a constant problem. We were fortunate in our particular group to have the manager of a large industrial company, the branch manager of a building society, and several others with either expert knowledge, or with contacts. During my time with the group we were successful in resettling several men back into society. The company manager, who was also a magistrate, took on several of these men in his business. They became reliable and trusted workers, and, to my knowledge, never let him down. This caring attitude was typical among members of the group, who were all involved in restoring relationships, finding accommodation for men about to be released, and giving other practical help. The women of the group supported the wives and families of the married prisoners in wives' group meetings. They also staffed the creche during visiting times, which enabled wives and girlfriends of prisoners to discuss their domestic affairs more privately. The after-care part of the work was as equally important as the actual custody visiting.

My contact with the probation service and with prisons has taught me that criminality cannot be attributed simply to personality defects. It has revealed to me greater depths of knowledge and understanding, not only about my own psychological responses, but about society in general, which may not have been discovered in any other way. I found that it was far too easy to dismiss the social and psychological pressures and tensions which contribute to the frightening criminal statistics in this and other countries. Exposure to the complexity of social factors renders us all vulnerable to misdemeanours of every kind during our lifetimes.

My experience as a probation volunteer has extended my adult education, for which I am thankful. For instance, I had not appreciated the significance of the strong link between social deprivation and crime and delinquency until I became involved as a volunteer. This was later verified by my academic studies. In a study of one

Lancashire town, I discovered that a high crime rate, unemployment and delinquency are closely linked with poor social conditions: low standards of health care, bad housing and low educational achievement. Often these factors could be traced in a pattern over several generations.

As a more experienced volunteer I was asked to befriend a prisoner named Jack in Wakefield top security prison. His offence was a serious one, but not uncommon. If his story is true, as he told it to me in dribs and drabs, there could have been mitigating circumstances which had not been taken into consideration at the time of his trial. He was a lonely man, intensely so, because he had been rejected by his family. Although he was a slightly older man than me, Jack and I had several things in common our wartime experience of army service, and our Lancastrian roots – which gave us something to talk about.

I only got to see Jack four or five times a year. Visits were arranged on a group basis, when two or three members of the group were travelling to visit other residents in Wakefield. In between we kept in contact by letter. Letters for prisoners at that time, however, were restricted to one or two per month, so communication between us was infrequent. I was probably his only contact outside the prison.

Like others I have known in Jack's situation, he often wrote or spoke of his pipedream of getting an old broken-down country cottage which he could do up, and a plot of land which he could cultivate. Seldom, if ever, does the symbolic dream come true, but there is a happy sequel to Jack's story.

He was discharged, and returned to his Lancashire home after four years in prison. Two or three days after his release I had an unusual telephone call. The caller asked me if I had been visiting someone in Wakefield prison. Naturally, I was a bit cautious in my reply, but when I was satisfied that the call was genuine I said that I might be able to help him if he could tell me why he was so interested. He then told me that Jack was his father, and he was anxious to know where he was. Quite truthfully, I told him that I had not got his father's address, but I could tell him that he intended to return to Lancashire.

Apparently this son of Jack's had recently had a genuine religious experience, which had changed his attitude towards his father. He said, 'I know he has done wrong, but he is still my dad, and I want to get things right between us before it is too late.' I like to think that Jack and his family are still together, and that he now has the support of his children and grandchildren.

There were several groups similar to our own – made up of ordinary people like myself – which met regularly in North Lancashire, trying to learn how best to help people to pick up the broken pieces of their shattered lives after several years in prison. These groups came together once a year in a Volunteers' Conference, representing all aspects of the work in which the Probation Service was involved, plus the volunteers.

After the reorganisation of the district boundaries in 1974, Chorley and South Ribble district formed its own group – Chorley and South Ribble Probation Volunteers – and I was asked to become its chairman. It was not an arduous task. Most of the day-to-day work was done by the full-time staff of the respective offices in Chorley and Leyland. The role of the chairman, as I saw it, was to facilitate visits, and to maintain the interest of the group by stimulating discussion on relevant topics. During my chairmanship it was the turn of the Chorley/Leyland group to host the annual Volunteers' Conference.

As chairman I had to chair the meeting – a daunting challenge for anyone, regardless of any visual difficulties. The meeting was to take place in Chorley Town Hall, and about 500 representatives were expected to attend. It was a full day conference with lunch and tea provided. We, the local committee, decided that the event would be in the form of a talk-in – an open discussion, based on a hypothetical case.

Four well-known persons connected with the judicial processes agreed to form a panel: a county court judge, the Assistant Chief Constable of Lancashire, a magistrate, and the organiser of a Victim Support Group, with myself as chairman. Unfortunately, the judge was involved in a road accident on his way to the conference and was unable to attend. He was replaced by another magistrate, which slightly altered the balance of the panel.

We had hoped for a stimulating open debate on current issues thrown up by the 'incident', with the full participation of the audience. From that point of view, we were not disappointed with the response, but it would be an understatement to say that it was lively and controversial. Before the meeting started I was apprehensive at the thought of taking charge, sitting between a senior judge and the Assistant Chief Constable, but before the proceedings got properly under way, I realised that my biggest problem would be coping with all the diverging attitudes and opinions on the subject of crime, punishment and penal reform – from the 'flog 'em and hang 'em' to the 'softly, softly' school of thought – and a barrage of awkward questions from the vociferous crowd in front of me. There were some very controversial views expressed from all over the large hall. I do not think that opinions were changed as a result of what had been said, but at least people had been given the opportunity to air their views in public, and that seemed to satisfy the majority. It was an experience I had first dreaded, but at the close of the meeting, and after a few plaudits, especially from the Assistant Chief Constable, I felt much better.

I had no desire to occupy the chairmanship for too long. At a convenient opportunity, after holding the office for several years, I handed over the chairmanship to another reluctant volunteer.

Early in 1970 I received a surprise telephone call from one of the local councillors who wanted to put my name forward as the local representative on the advisory council of the new BBC Radio Blackburn, which was then being set up. The station was due to come into operation the following year. It was an honour to be considered for the job, but I was puzzled as to why I should have been the local authority's nominee for the post, until it was pointed out that, as a blind person already in contact with the public, and more dependent on radio for information and entertainment than most other people, I was thought to be an appropriate candidate. Without knowing fully what the job entailed I agreed to let my name go forward.

In due course I received confirmation of the appointment from the then Postmaster-General, John Stonehouse, shortly before he attempted his mysterious disappearing act. Radio Blackburn began broadcasting from its studios, then a converted garage and service station in King Street, Blackburn, on 26th January 1971. The advisory council comprised about 20 people, representing a wide spectrum of interests: industrial, religious, cultural, educational, and minority groups. Public service broadcasting was new to most of us on the council, so it was natural that there would be much interest and excitement at the prospect of having a broadcasting station on our doorstep, and becoming involved at the start of this new enterprise.

The main function of this advisory body was to be a channel of communication between the station and the public, and to bring to the attention of the manager our observations and those of other people referred to us. We were free to criticise programmes and general presentation, and to make suggestions about the introduction of new programmes, especially those of major local interest. Meetings of the advisory council took place six times a year.

I was four years old when I heard my first radio transmission. A playmate and I were visiting one of his uncles who was twiddling the knobs on a 'cat's whisker' when I heard music which, I was told, was coming from London. My fascination with radio broadcasting continued as a schoolboy, when I played around with an improvised microphone, trying to broadcast through the radio set in the living-room from a contraption in the kitchen. Until I entered the studios of BBC Radio Blackburn, however, I had only the slenderest connection with live broadcasting and broadcasters – some of my battalion colleagues were '30-minute celebrities' when they went on the air on All India Radio during the war. Since the advent of local radio, taking part in a radio programme has become commonplace to a number of people, and has lost most of its terror.

When the time came for me to make my first broadcast on BBC Radio Blackburn, however, the fascination was swamped by nerves; it was far more daunting than I had expected.

16

My four-year stint with BBC Radio Blackburn coincided with my introduction to the Open University and the start of my academic career. We moved house at the end of 1970 when opportunities for study appeared more rewarding than my prospects in poultry. I more or less severed my connections with poultry farming, but I kept up my participation in other fields: preaching and pastoral work, probation and prison visiting and voluntary home teaching.

At the age of 49 I embarked on a study programme which I hoped would earn me a Bachelor of Arts degree. There was a great contrast in the switch from the mainly physical occupation on a smallholding to learning how to get to grips with an extensive university course. Hour after hour would have to be spent poring over text books, and attending lectures and seminars, most likely with men and women much younger than myself. It may have seemed madness for anyone to go for a university degree in later middle-age. It was considered even more ridiculous by some of my contemporaries for me to attempt it with the added disadvantages of blindness and a head injury, to say nothing of my elementary education. But in no way was I going to miss the only chance I had to get on to the academic ladder after so many abortive efforts.

The concept of distance learning by means of radio and television and a network of local centres, had by the end of the 1960s become established as The Open University. When the project was announced it seemed the ideal system of learning for someone in my position. It offered degrees in higher education to anyone, regardless of previous educational experience. It was advertised as an opportunity for the physically disabled with little previous educational background, to enter the field of higher learning, for whom it was hoped to provide special facilities. The main qualification for entry was a strong motivation to learn, and provided that the candidate obtained the six minimum credits over an unspecified period of time he would qualify for a Bachelor's degree. As soon as the prospectuses were available I got a copy and sent off my application form without delay.

It was obvious that competition for places would be fierce. In the first year 32,000 applications were expected for 12,000 places. It was understood that some preference would be given to disabled applicants, but this was no guarantee that they would get in. Before I was accepted my potential and suitability were assessed, at home, by a senior member of the University's admissions department. Among the 12,000 undergraduates accepted in January 1971, there were just 12 blind students – a ratio of a thousand to one – and that is how I calculated my chances of getting over the hurdle of my first year's study.

It was only when my place was confirmed by post that the scale of the commitment I was making began to sink in, and I wondered if I would have the stamina to cope. This would impose sacrifices and discipline, not only upon myself, but also, especially, on Nancey. Inevitably, she would be the one most intimately involved – even more than she had been before. I would be more dependent upon her eyes for most of the visual content of the studies ahead.

Confirmation of my place on the Open University course came after two or three weeks, and with it yet another identification number to be added to the long list of numbers by which I could be traced. I was now student A0229609. It was another string of numbers which would become indelibly imprinted on my brain, just like my army and war pensions number, and even the Co-op number which I still retain from my childhood. I was now a member of yet another organisation with my own identity tag.

The Royal National Institute for the Blind was invited to co-operate with the university in providing back-up facilities for their blind undergraduates. They agreed to participate in a pilot scheme which involved preparing all the information about the Arts Foundation Course, and all the additional required reading.

Things were pretty chaotic for everyone at the outset of my studies, especially for Nancey and myself, as we were still getting acquainted with our new home. I started my duties at Radio Blackburn at the same time, and these had also to be fitted in with my other responsibilities. The Open University also had teething problems of its own, without the extra ones produced by its visually handicapped students.

The student section of the British Talking Book Service did a stupendous job, and all credit is due to Miss Urquhart, the chief librarian, and Mr Garrard Green, the actor and professional reader, who read nearly everything that had to be read on to tape. How they managed to complete everything on time is nothing short of a miracle. The RNIB also prepared charts, diagrams and other documents in a tactile format, which was a great help. In spite of these resources, I thought it necessary to buy all the required text books in printed format as a back-up, and so that Nancey could keep a check on the course – a 'pair of braces' in addition to the 'belt' and 'elastic'.

My fear was that I would never get through the work in time, and I began to wonder how I would cope with the specified reading, and then get through the written assignment, which was due within a month or so from the opening date. We were still not properly settled in our new house when I started the course. The room I intended to use as a study had been used as a cocktail lounge by the previous owner, and was still cluttered with a fitted bar complete with fairy lights and high bar stools. There was just about room for an old dining table which I could use as a writing desk, but all my books, and Talking Book cassettes, found a temporary home on the floor. If I had thoughts of quitting, it would have been now.

The Open University was different in many ways from its conventional counterparts, in size, teaching methods and administration. At its launch it was considerably larger than any conventional British university. Its main base was in the newly-created town of Milton Keynes, Buckinghamshire. The individual student was linked to the university through one of six regional offices, and a network of study centres located in most of the larger towns and cities throughout the country. The regional office for the north west was in Manchester, where staff were under the direction of the Regional Director. The network of study centres, teaching staff and administrators had their own distinctive responsibilities, and the study centre was regarded as the basic and most indispensable unit of the Open University system by many of its students. Each student was assigned to a counsellor, and it was at the study centre that he or she was most likely to be found.

The Open University had foreseen the value of counselling as part of its teaching programme, but this part of the system had its problems in the beginning. Unfortunately, the counsellor to whom I was assigned was unaware that one of his group was blind; he was as new as I was to the Open University, and had no previous experience of dealing with blind students. He was perplexed when I presented myself at the first group meeting, but things soon improved once these initial snags were sorted out. However, right to the very end of my time with the OU, I felt that the problems of blind students were not fully appreciated, though at least, the counselling system meant that there was someone at hand locally with whom to talk through one's problems.

Students doing similar courses formed themselves into self-help discussion groups, which were immensely valuable, especially to me with my own special need. It was in these small groups that many of us who were making a restart in education gained more confidence and self-assurance, realising that we were not alone in facing difficult academic problems. I soon began to feel less uncomfortable among the group, many of whom were already in academic positions or professional occupations. It was comforting at times to realise that many of my fellow students were as baffled as I was in coming to grips with certain aspects of the course. It was even more encouraging when tutor-marked assignments were returned with good grades and favourable comments, though it was a different story when the grade wasn't as good as I was expecting. Telephone messages were soon being exchanged between students, as assignments were returned and we discussed our grades.

The main event of the student's year was the Summer School, which was a compulsory part of most courses of the OU syllabus. The Summer Schools were located on the campuses of several red-brick universities during the main vacation. It was in this experience, according to many of my contemporaries, that the Open University really came alive. Until then, most of the teaching had been done at a distance, where the individual struggled in isolation; now he had the chance to meet some of those who had prepared the course units and marked his assignments. For me it was a boost to meet with the people, who until then had been voices or names on the radio and television support programmes. Provision was made for disabled students to have a personal assistant at the expense of the university. As several others from my own local group were attending the same Summer School at Keele University, I thought that I would not require any other help. In retrospect I did manage, but no doubt it would have been much simpler had Nancey been there.

It was surprising to realise how quickly the academic year had passed. From January to October I had slogged and sweated as I prepared for the examination at the end of October. Ten hours' work a week had been the recommended minimum on each course, but in my case it amounted to almost twice or three times that amount including listening to the associated radio and television programmes. Even then I felt that I had not done justice to the assignment. I had coped with most of the first year's work for the Arts Foundation Course reasonably well. By the end of September most of the course had been completed, and the bulk of the assignments had been marked and returned. I had obtained well above the average grades so far in the continuous assessments, but even with all this to my credit there was no room for complacency. I could still come unstuck at the last hurdle: the end-of-course examination. For me, at the age of almost 50, it represented the most critical educational test of my life.

Special arrangements were made for me to sit the examination at home with an invigilator present. As a blind student I had three options: typewriting, Braille or the use of an amanuensis. I had to state my preference at least two months prior to the examination, not an easy decision to make so far in advance. None of them was equivalent to being able to sit at a desk along with other candidates, scan the questions, and get on with the paper in a normal way. Even with a discretionary time allowance of an additional ten minutes per hour, I still felt at a disadvantage. I did not fancy a repetition of my experience when I applied for the Home Teacher of The Blind Course in Leeds. For that reason I discounted using my typewriter. Writing Braille continuously for over three hours, with a Perkins Brailler, is physically and mentally tiring. It requires concentration, not only for answering the question, but also for the formation of letters and words – the slightest misplaced dot can change the spelling of a word, or even the sense of a phrase or sentence. Even the additional time allowance does not compensate for the extra strain and sheer physical energy. In the end I chose the use of an amanuensis, who would also act as my invigilator. This was the least unsatisfactory option of the three methods but I was not completely at ease, whatever method I chose to use.

I nearly missed sitting the examination altogether. The morning of the exam was a beautiful autumn morning, bright and crisp. To relieve the tension that was building up inside me, I decided to take a walk by myself in

Worden Park, which is not too far from where we live. Nancey offered to come with me, but this was one occasion when I wanted to be alone for a while. It was not too far, and I was sure that I could find my way around the park unaided, as long as I kept close to the hard, gravel paths. Unfortunately, when I deviated from the path trying to cut a corner near the duck pond, I somehow missed picking up the path again. Until then I had not realised that the park was so vast, and that I could go so far without coming to a fence or pathway. There was hardly a sound from any direction. I called out for help, but there was no response.

I felt more anxious, and not a little frightened, as the time passed. There were no clues to give me any idea of my whereabouts. By now Nancey would be getting anxious, wondering what might have happened, as I had been away much longer than I had intended. Eventually, after what seemed an age, I was rescued by a park ranger who led me to the gate by which I had entered the park. Nancey was so relieved to see me coming along the road that she almost burst into tears and, probably with some justification, delivered a strong lecture. I thought a solitary stroll prior to the exam would assist the flow of adrenaline – it certainly did, but not in the way I'd expected!

Whether the mental fog which descended upon me as I started my exam was due to my wanderings in the park, or just exam nerves, is hard to say. All that I do know is that I seemed to be in a 'blue funk' all the way through the test.

The results were not due out until after Christmas, which seemed a long time to wait. When the pressure was off, and there were no text books or course units to study, or assignments to write, it was a strange sensation – trying to slow down the momentum and return to a normal family life. On one of those anticlimactic days between Christmas and New Year, my results came through, but I was almost too scared to let Nancey open the envelope.

After fingering it for several minutes I allowed her to reveal its contents. I was still shaking with emotions of hope and fear – and then disbelief when Nancey announced that I had passed with credit, my first major educational success since my poultry husbandry qualification. There was much more to do before I could claim that coveted BA degree, but at last I was on my way. It was a wonderful belated Christmas present and the best encouragement I could have to proceed to the next part of the course.

17

My success, as thrilling as it was to me, represented only one sixth of my degree course and only one eighth of the full honours degree, which I fully intended to aim for. At the rate of one full-credit course a year it was going to take me some considerable time. It was for this reason that I wanted to get my degree within four years, taking an additional two years to complete the honours degree course. I was then nearly 50, and I could not be sure what physical condition I might be in so far ahead; I set my sights accordingly.

My plans was to take two full-credit courses in the year ahead, and one full-credit and one half-credit course in the following two years. In the two subsequent years I would have to complete two higher level courses in order to qualify for an honours degree. I had been asked to state my course preferences for my second year whilst I was still plodding through my initial course, regardless of the result, and I was now committed to the challenging prospect of completing two full-credit courses in the next ten months. As an undergraduate, without any exemptions, it was compulsory that one of the full-credit courses still to be undertaken should be in the Foundation category.

The RNIB Student Tape Library was then already preparing the recorded material for the foundation course for the social sciences, so it seemed sensible to make this one of my choices. For my other course that year I opted to do the second level course: The Reformation and Renaissance, for which I would need to make my own arrangements for reading the set books and the course units. I would now be working concurrently in two faculties of the university – Arts and Social Sciences. Doing the two courses in parallel meant that I would have double the assignments to get through, besides attending twice the previous number of seminars and study groups. Nancey, too, would have much more reading to do, even than before. But by balancing out my course work between the Arts and Social Sciences I felt that I could more easily keep on top of things. It would be less fatiguing to be able to switch from one subject to the other when I reached a mental block.

The course on the Renaissance and Reformation covered the art, literature, religion, science and the political intrigues of the 14th and 15th centuries. All aspects and cultural developments in Europe were considered from an interactive historical viewpoint. These subjects were taught by specialist members of Open University staff and outside lecturers in seminars in different parts of the region. This comprehensive system of learning stimulated and challenged me. Even the visual content of the course, such as architecture and paintings, which, of course, I could not see, became more intelligible and meaningful to me by imaginative presentation. There was an advantage in these comprehensive studies, and I did not feel myself too much deprived.

The Social Science foundation course concentrated on five main areas: sociology, politics, economics, psychology and spatial geography. Each of these subjects formed the groundwork of specialised courses in higher levels of study. In several instances there was an overlap between the Arts course and the Social Science course, which I found helpful in understanding some particular concept in one or other of the disciplines. Often, when I was baffled by a problem in my Social Science studies, I found some illumination from the work I had been doing in the Arts course, and vice versa. Both courses were equally demanding.

I was greatly relieved to learn that Garrard Green would again be used by the Student Talking Book Library to record the essential documents of the course. His invaluable contribution would take some of the pressure away from Nancey, who would have plenty to do with reading for the Renaissance and Reformation course. As long as I could rely on the reading service, and my wife for the extra reading and as my personal assistant at the

Summer School, I was fairly confident that I could cope with the work.

I was as self-critical of my work then as I had been in my first year, and more concerned about its quality now that I had comparable standards to maintain. Many academic scientists are sceptical about the rigour of social science studies as an exact science, but coming to it new, as I did, it challenged many previously held assumptions, and caused me to examine every part of my social existence from a more analytical perspective. Whereas before, I had taken for granted the integration of the various strands and structures of society, I was now analysing more closely what I was hearing and reading.

Time was always at a premium during the year. I still had my preaching and my other voluntary commitments, which were high priorities. Luckily, there was nothing serious to disrupt my progress, though inevitably there were frequent snags and frustrating delays, usually associated with the arrival of course material. In spite of this and the heavier workload, it was a fairly successful year as far as I was concerned. I could not claim that I did equally well in all my assignments, although I was disappointed when I got anything less than a C grade.

By the time of the examination in the autumn I still had misgivings about it, and was wondering which of the three exam options would suit me best. The amanuensis had not been very satisfactory in my last exam. After some thought, I decided to use my faithful Imperial portable typewriter, and hope that I would make a better job of it than I did on that fateful day in Leeds a few years before. This time I had the invigilator beside me to give me clues about my position when making alterations and corrections. It was not easy but at least I found it much better than I thought it would be. When it was over there were some reassuring noises from my invigilator about the way he thought it had gone, but I dared not relax until the results were published at the end of the year.

I sighed with relief when I learned that I had gained two passes at Merit level. Now, after two years' study, I was halfway to my degree, and I felt able to approach the remainder of the course with growing confidence. It was still my intention to complete the course within four years, and I got ready to start The Age of Revolutions arts course to give me one full credit, and Sociological Perspectives to give me another half credit. This would maintain a balance between the Arts and Social Sciences. It was another heavy study load, especially as these courses did not have the full backing of the Talking Book Library service.

The Age of Revolutions covered the years between 1776 and 1830, studying the military and political revolutions in Europe and America, and the industrial, technological and social developments of the time. The course brought everything about the period into a concentrated focus, making it possible to obtain a representative picture of life at a particular moment in time.

It was a valuable experience to have the benefit of some of the leading authorities sharing their knowledge and experience of their own specialised subject, and something that must make the Open University a unique learning institution. Possibly for the first time in my life I was getting a taste of academic education at its best. The courses I was now studying were a serious challenge to many of my comfortable assumptions, especially regarding religion and my Christian faith.

Neither of my new courses had a Summer School. This was made up for by extended regional tutorials and seminars. As these were located in scattered venues in the north west I would have been unable to attend them had it not been for the help from my fellow students who provided the transport. I may add that this arrangement was often to the mutual benefit of my colleagues, because they often depended on my navigational skill to get us to our destination – the skill of holding mental maps in my head dates back many years. I believe that being with other students in this way was a major contribution to my ultimate success. The tutorial element of the courses was not compulsory, but as a student working in isolation, these face-to-face meetings with specialists were the best chances I had of acquiring knowledge and further information.

In spite of my deprivation of sight I was fascinated with the visual art content of the Age of Revolutions course, so I decided to visit London and find out a bit more about the exhibits in the National Gallery and other places which were constantly being referred to in the course material. Nancey, of course, had to describe the details to me, but now that I was in my third year with the OU, I was more knowledgeable about the history of art. Nancey, too, began to take an interest in the subject.

By this time I was almost an OU addict. My aim was still the coveted BA, but the acquisition of knowledge for its own sake was equally important to me. My appetite had been whetted and I was curious to learn more about the subjects to which I had been introduced. Soaking up Open University material like a sponge, the more I learned, the more eager I became.

At the end of the course I still had reservations about the examination. The arrangements had not changed. This year I chose the Braille option, using my Perkins Brailler, hoping that I might be more comfortable than I had been with the alternatives in previous years, but I was even less happy with the result. I was granted the usual ten minutes an hour extension for each paper, but as I had already pointed out to the examination authorities, it was something of a dubious concession, as it only added to the stress I was under. The Perkins Brailler is an excellent machine, but I did not realise the amount of physical effort it would take to operate the machine for over three hours without a break. I knew from the start that I was likely to make simple spelling mistakes and would have difficulty in correcting them. I reached a stage when I was so busy concentrating on my subjects that I was forgetting all that I knew about Braille rules.

Of the two exams, The Age of Revolutions and Sociological Perspectives, I was most confident of a high mark in the latter; it was a course I had thoroughly enjoyed. Amongst other topics it dealt with the sociology of religion, in which I had very good assignment results. However, when the results came out at the end of the year I had passed The Age of Revolutions with credit, but there was no mention of my sociology results. A few days later I was called to undergo an extra viva voce exam at the Preston Study Centre – no reason was given. It probably meant that I was a borderline case between a Distinction and a Pass, or between a Pass and a Fail, which I found hard to understand. I could only deduce that there was some problem with my written Braille paper. It was a great load off my mind when confirmation of a successful pass arrived a few days afterwards, but I was going to think carefully before I used Braille again for sitting exams.

In my first year with OU I was asked to contribute an article to *Open View*, a student's magazine compiled and published students from the north west. My article was called 'A Thousand to One'. In it I likened my university experience to that of taking part in a horse-race with many hurdles to get over, and myself as a thousand-to-one finisher. After three years I was still in the field, but the odds against me reaching the finishing post were shortening as the months passed.

The number of courses being made accessible to blind students through the Student Tape Library was steadily increasing and the options now open to me in my fourth and final year (excluding honours) were bewilderingly numerous. A new half-credit course which particularly appealed to me was The Early Roman Empire and the Rise of Christianity. This seemed an obvious choice for someone already acquainted with the subject. To maintain a balance between the Arts and Social Sciences I opted for Decision-making in Britain, a full-credit course. This was an intensive exploration into the various forms of decision-making in governmental and public organis-ations and institutions. It touched on almost every aspect of public life, from agriculture to the nationalised industries plus the health service and law and order. Luckily, this course was fully supported by the Student Tape Library. The reading list for the course was extensive, as may be imagined, so there was not much let-up for Nancey, especially as I also needed some help with The Early Roman Empire and the Rise of Christianity course.

At the beginning of the year I met up again with colleagues from previous courses and new self-help groups were soon established. For me, these were an essential part of the OU support structure. It was like a game of musical chairs on a large scale – students reshuffling themselves into small packs for study and discussion, hoping to spark off new lines of thought. As before, lifts to the various venues were willingly offered to me. With this backup, and with the unfailing support of my wife, I would have been extremely disappointed if I had failed to make the grade in this crucial year.

Of course, I had still seven hours of written examinations to overcome, which was always an unknown factor, and when it came I still had the same qualms about it. But to my delight, and that of the family and all those who had helped me, I had made the mountain peak. It was a quietly satisfying, rather than an exuberant, experience to hear that I had 'made it', but it was another few months before I donned my academic gown for the first time.

18

I was 54 when I was awarded a Bachelor of Arts degree. University degrees were uncommon acquisitions in the Taylor family, so mine attracted some publicity, and one or two commendations from far and near. I cannot say that I did not appreciate the general adulation, but I was glad when all the fuss died down, and I was allowed to become my normal self once again. I was pleased to be one of the first blind graduates of the Open University; it showed that it was now possible for people like myself to study at this level.

I could not afford to dwell too long on the congratulations I received, when there was so much studying still to be done. I was determined not to let my achievement go to my head, even though I was now Tom Taylor, BA. Before this I had tended to regard anyone with letters after their name as intellectually superior, but now that I was in this position myself I felt even more ignorant than I did before!

My sights were already set on an honours degree before I had confirmation of my pass at ordinary level, so I was in no position to relax. Two further credits in third-level subjects were needed to make me an honours graduate. The honours category would partly depend on the grades I had already attained, and partly on the results of these two extra years.

In anticipation of my success I enrolled for the course The 19th Century Novel and its Legacy. The prescribed reading included a formidable list of 19th and early 20th century classics, and I was impatient to get started. The course traced the development of the novel from the later 18th century onwards, in Europe and America.

Studying such an extensive range of authors in depth has sharpened my critical faculty, which makes it hard for me, even today, to enjoy many modern novels. Very few modern authors are able to move me as did George Eliot's

Middlemarch, and Tolstoy's *Anna Karenina* and to a lesser extent Virginia Woolf's *Mrs Dalloway* with their 'stream of consciousness' perspective. In addition to Dickens, George Eliot, Charlotte Brönte, Tolstoy and other celebrated authors like Mark Twain, there were studies of Balzac, Zola and Turgenev. If the objective was to sharpen my critical faculty for reading novels, it was certainly effective. It was an absorbing and stimulating study, which completely transformed my attitude towards all kinds of literature.

The degree ceremony for my group took place in the Free Trade Hall, Manchester, on a warm, sunny Saturday afternoon in spring. For a few hours we took our noses from the grindstone to enjoy our academic success of the previous year. The pavements around the Free Trade Hall were congested with new university graduates in their black gowns and blue and gold hoods. These were not the usual exuberant youngsters, fresh from their halls of residence, but a concourse of older men and women, displaying their newly-acquired status with justifiable pride.

With such a large number of graduates eligible to attend the ceremony, some restriction had to be imposed on the number of relatives and friends allowed to attend. The selection was made by ballot, and I was allocated two seats for guests. Neither Nancey nor I would have been too disappointed if we had not been present, but possibly my mother would have taken it  badly if she had been denied this unique family occasion: her son receiving a university degree.

A problem I was anticipating was, 'How am I going to cope with the platform procedure without attracting too much attention to my blindness?' I need not have worried! It had all been discreetly arranged beforehand that this part of the ceremony should be done as inconspicuously as possible. When my turn came, someone, I presume it was a member of staff, guided me to shake hands with the Chancellor. It had been requested by the university that there should be no applauding of individual graduates. That rule had been kept until I was shaking hands with the Chancellor, when there was a spontaneous outburst of cheering and clapping from the body of the hall and the platform party, but I was too engrossed in what I was doing to realise that the applause had anything to do with me. It was only when it was mentioned later that I fully appreciated what had happened

As we returned to Bury in the taxi to drop off my mother, I recalled my school-days at Elton Council School, and wondered what might have happened to my classmates and teachers in the intervening years. I would like to have shared this day with them. This was where the roots of my education lay, and at that moment I was deeply appreciative of all those who had been instrumental in my early education; my old headmaster, E W Wright, and Miss Hesketh, one of my form teachers. Two of my former junior school teachers, Miss Kitchen and Miss Smith, whom I met from time to time, claimed some of the credit for my award, and took pride and pleasure in telling the story.

The Summer School for my course that year took place at York University, and for several reasons remains one of the highlights of my years with the Open University. The environment of the campus, the special arrangements for disabled students, and the perfect summer weather all combined to make it seem more like a holiday than a concentrated study period. Nevertheless, the atmosphere was conducive to learning. Professional actors were in attendance to dramatise excerpts from the novel which helped to imprint them more indelibly in my memory.

I have had a soft spot for York since I was stationed there during the war, and this reminiscence made this return visit even more enjoyable. The campus at York was comparatively new. The ornamental lake, and its attendant duck population makes York one of the more scenic of the modern universities. Our living accommodation touched the water's edge, so Nancey could observe the waterfowl at close quarters, when she was not escorting or helping me.

Nancey had only recently passed her driving test, and was a bit hesitant about undertaking a long journey with little experience. However, after she had scrutinised the road map, and placed some reliance on my knowledge of the route from my service days, we set off in our black Morris Minor – gleaming brightly after its extra polish for the occasion. The journey could not have been better until we got into the city centre. I was familiar with the road layout as it had been in 1940, and was convinced that I could direct Nancey to where we ought to be. I had not made allowance for present day conditions, and also I was ignorant of the fact that a regatta and festival were taking place, and that the city would be chock-a-block with vehicles. When we got mixed up with the traffic in the city centre and were confronted with traffic diversions, I was thrown off my stride and Nancey began to panic a bit because I could not tell her immediately which way to go. I assumed that we were being diverted on to the Fulford road, which I well remembered, so I told Nancey to keep going, and all was well. Our black Morris rested in the car park, and when we were ready to drive off after two weeks on the campus, the shining black car was thick with dust, and resembled a camouflaged jeep ready for war service. As we left the outskirts of York the skies blackened, the rain came down in torrents, and did not stop until we were well across the Lancashire boundary. Driving home in bad visibility was more than an adequate test of Nancey's driving ability.

I ought to have got over the nervous anticipation of taking Open University examinations by this time, but I was still as apprehensive as ever when the seventh and penultimate examination came round in October, but when the results were out I was glad to know that I had chalked up another credit – it was now 'seven down, one to go'. I was now set ready for the final stretch. It had taken me five years to get to this point! It seemed to justify the remarks on one of my school reports, written by Miss Hesketh, my form teacher, 'Tom has the ability to persevere.'

I had already made a provisional start on my final course: a newly-introduced course on Social Psychology. The grade of my Honours degree depended on the outcome of this final course, and I was prepared to give it all I had, in hopes of a good degree. Social psychology was one of the themes in the Social Science foundation course, and was a subject in which I had become increasingly interested. It also had some relevance for me as a preacher, pastoral worker, voluntary worker with the probation service, and prison visitor, with its treatment of personal and group behaviour and the motivations underlying social control and development.

Social psychology brought me face to face with my own personality, and taught me how to explore my attitudes and opinions. Tracing the sources of these was not always a comfortable exercise but it also gave me a deeper appreciation of the behavioural patterns in other people. Even though I could not condone the conduct of some of the offenders I met through the probation service – the outcasts and rejects of society – studying the course material gave me a better understanding of what made them tick.

There was no Summer School requirement, but each student had to undertake a psychological project of substantial proportions, which had to be completed before the end of the course. I opted for The Kelly Repertory Grid method of personality analysis, a system constructed from a matrix of personality types, matched against a scale of attitudes. By means of a computer calculation it was possible to assess the strengths and weaknesses of an individual's personality traits. This was my first encounter with the mysteries of the computer, at a time when modern computers were in their infancy. Communication with it was by means of coded forms sent through the post to the Computer Centre at the Open University's headquarters in Milton Keynes. When it is remembered that the process had to be repeated several times to complete an analysis, it shows how things have moved forward in the past few years. The system has its uses for diagnostic purposes; it caused me to face some of the realities in myself, and from that point of view it was worthwhile.

Thanks to my tutor, Dr Jerry Foster, the course and the project went well, and all that mattered now was the outcome of my final exam; the value of my degree would ultimately depend on it. I was hopeful that I would finish off my six years with a worthwhile degree. I was, therefore, especially delighted to hear that I had been awarded an upper second class honours degree. Students were only permitted to attend one award ceremony, either the ordinary or the honours. As I had already been presented, this was something I did not have to bother about.

It took time to realise that I had actually come to the end of my studies with the Open University. The withdrawal symptoms were almost as painful as the studies had been, and it seemed very strange not to be working on an assignment, or some academic research. All my assignments from the beginning of the course were carefully filed away, including my rough notes.

For the majority of the students the obtaining of a degree meant some improvement in their prospects, either by promotion or more money, but this did not affect me. However, I was occupied in voluntary service as a preacher, a pastoral visitor and probation volunteer. The money side of it was not important to me, as long as I had the satisfaction of knowing that I was making a contribution to the general welfare of society. This was not a one-way process. I had realised for many years that I had been the recipient of much help; now it was my turn to give what help I could and use the knowledge I had acquired in my voluntary work. Nevertheless, tangible encouragement came a few weeks later, in the form of a cheque for £100. The National Westminster Bank presented me with this prize, which they were awarding that year to the most successful disabled student.

At this moment my concern was 'What should my next move be?' The solution came a few months later in a chance meeting with a member of the staff of Lancaster University, at a church conference. In our conversations, between the sessions of the conference, we discussed the opportunities of study for a Master's Degree at Lancaster University. He thought that one of the courses, Behaviour in Organisations, would meet my requirements. With his encouragement, and the offer of an introduction to the head of the appropriate department, I returned to Leyland with a bit more idea of my future.

19

My introduction to Lancaster University was made with as much blissful ignorance of what I was letting myself in for, as my introduction to the Open University had been several years before, and with no less trepidation. My self-assurance forsook me as I made my way to the university hoping to study for a postgraduate degree. Stuart, my fellow Methodist and a tutor at Lancaster, had made the initial contact for me with the Behaviour in Organisations department, as he had promised to do. It was arranged for me to meet Professor Sylvia Shimmin, the head of the department, to discuss the preliminaries and the various options available to me.

I was like a schoolboy going to a new school for the first time, a bit apprehensive and unsure of myself. I did not know what to expect, or what would be expected of me, and how I would cope with this challenging adventure. At that stage I did not know what I was going to read. According to the syllabus I had several choices, depending on the type and level of degree.

The courses being offered in the Behaviour in Organisations department varied from a one-year taught course for a Master of Arts to a PhD of unspecified duration. In between these, there was an assortment of degrees. Some courses required full-time attendance at the university, whilst others could be done externally, on a part-time basis. The first thing I needed to sort out was what I was going to do in more specific terms. Once this was done, there would be no apparent obstacles to my progress, provided that I could obtain the necessary finance and that my application was accepted.

I had not visited the campus of Lancaster University until now, and I was not at all impressed by my initial visit. It was bleak, cold and windy on that October day in 1977 when Nancey and I parked our Morris in the extensive grounds. On that first occasion there seemed to be endless miles of cloistered alleyways, and corridors, passages and steps, going in all directions. The university consists of a conglomeration of buildings of various dimensions, linked to a main alleyway known as The Spine. We found the Behaviour in Organisations department located at the end of a twisting corridor on the fourth storey of one of the buildings linked to The Spine.

We had to wait for a few minutes before we were shown into the professor's room. As I waited with Nancey in the small annex, she told me that the walls were covered with posters and announcements, typical of a school or college, advertising the events and services available to staff and students. I was to become very familiar with this little corner of the university over the next four years!

By the end of my first interview with Professor Shimmin which lasted about an hour, I had learned that studying organisational behaviour was far more complicated than I had been led to believe from my brush with the subject in my Open University studies, and as she remarked, 'It can be a very messy business at the start.' Although my previous work had been a good introduction, for a thorough grasp of the subject I would need to know more about the varying schools of thought and differing approaches.

There was a lot to be done before I could complete the application form. After weighing up the pros and cons for a few days, I considered that my best option would be to do some original research on a topic with which I was already familiar, either the Church or the Probation Service. The preliminaries took me more than a month to sort out. I also had to make some inquiries about the availability of relevant resources as well as my own personal finance, and any required back-up I would need.

It was made clear from the start that my work would have to stand on its own merits, without any sympathy regarding my physical disability. This was something for which I was prepared, nor would I have wanted it any other way. It had always been my understanding with

Open University work, and I was as eager as anyone to prove, if only to myself, that I could complete this work given a reasonable opportunity.

My first idea was to concentrate on the organisational functioning of the Methodist Church, which had just then undergone a process of restructuring. This had to be abandoned partly because the new organisation was not yet properly established, which would make it difficult to assess its value. There were also some doubts about the accessibility of the necessary information. The immensity of the task had also to be taken into consideration for someone whose resources were very much restricted.

I then considered the possibility of looking at the local ecumenical situation. An inclusive organisation representing most of the Christian denominations in Leyland, known as the Leyland Churches Fellowship, had then existed for a number of years. To conduct a viable study of this organisation I would need some kind of authorisation, and I wondered what response there might be to my request from the clergy and ministers of the town. To do a thorough study I would have to have access to appropriate meetings and documents, and there is always the tendency in any research of this kind to arouse suspicions about motives and objectives. Although ecumenical relationships in Leyland had been on a formal constitutional base since the Fellowship was formed in 1968, very little was known about its operation outside its limited membership. I knew of its existence, and though I was ignorant about its constitution and the way it worked, I felt that it would make a suitable subject for academic study.

I next had an interview at Lancaster with the newly-appointed admissions tutor, Dr Bob Cooper. As I entered his room for the first time he was very apologetic about its disorderly state. This benign confession, however, was in sharp contrast to the devastating criticism he levelled at me when I submitted my first essay to him shortly afterwards. From then on I knew that getting this degree was not going to be a pushover. Such was my introduction into academic life at Lancaster University. I was left in no doubt that sweat and blood would be extracted from me before I had finished! More than once in those early years at Lancaster I returned home wondering if I would ever make the grade. I was discovering the truth of Professor Shimmin's remark, that all research starts out as a messy business.

Most of the existing research on Organisational Behaviour referred to political or business organisations, and there was very little of any value on church-based organisations. In the absence of practical models, it was a case of starting almost from scratch, using what knowledge I had from other disciplines. I would also need a supervisor within the department who was sufficiently knowledgeable about church-based organisations. Professor Shimmin, the head of the department, a fellow Methodist, agreed to act as my supervisor. Unfortunately she was due to take a year's sabbatical leave whilst my study was in progress, which I thought might disrupt things for a while. During that time I was supervised by Dr Bob Cooper, which probably worked to my advantage, for during his tutelage I was introduced to more extensive reading on the subject, and because he himself did not have a church background, I was compelled to be more explicit in my exposition.

My intention, as I indicated in my application, was to do a research degree at PhD level, but on the advice of Professor Shimmin this was scaled down to a less ambitious MSc, which it would be easy enough to upgrade if the quality of my work warranted it. The university had specified a minimum of two and a maximum of five years for the completion of the project. If I paced myself properly I could probably complete the degree in under four years, allowing for contingencies; it actually took me just under four years to the final typing and binding of my work.

For my own convenience, I began by producing a tactile representational model of the Leyland Churches Fellowship, based on a biological concept which I extracted from the literature on poultry husbandry which I had read several years before. Although the analogy could not be carried too far there were sufficient similarities between the structural functions of a domestic fowl and the behavioural functions of a social organisation to provide me with an initial working model. Both consist of similar interrelated systems: inputs, outputs and interactions. I visualised the Fellowship as a small, complex, dynamic organism of interconnecting systems not unlike those of a chicken: digestive, circulatory, reproductive, to name just a few.

Before I could begin to assemble and analyse my data – the attitudes and opinions of its members – I had to set the study in a contextual framework. This was a mammoth task in itself; I had to delve into the social history of the town, and explore the background details of all the churches in the Fellowship. I was also recommended to read numerous text books from the University library, to widen my knowledge, and as most of these were only available in print Nancey had the laborious task of reading them on to tape. Local historians and library assistants supplied me with archive material.

To get a comparative perspective between what the Fellowship set out to do, and what had been achieved over the years, I proposed to talk to a number of clerical and lay members who had been involved in it since its formation. With their permission, I recorded their answers on a small, unobtrusive tape recorder. Each interview had then to be transcribed before it could be analysed and interpreted for the scrutiny of my supervisor. The interview procedure was probably the most difficult part of the four-year programme. It took me several weeks to cover the series of interviews, which took place on a one-to-one basis. In most cases I had to give an assurance that the study was strictly for research purposes, and that confidences would be respected. Most of the respondents were forthcoming although some were more cautious.

As this was an external degree my visits to the Lancaster campus were only made at essential points. It became essential to see my supervisor more often in the final stages, when I was completing my thesis; minor problems could be solved by a telephone call to the department at any time. It was up to me to keep up with the timetable I had set myself; no one expected anything else from me.

After nearly four years' work, which had taken me along an upwards, gruelling path, with many diversions, false trails and blind alleys – to say nothing of my personal frustrations – I was ready to submit my thesis for examination. Disaster almost struck on the very day I was about to deliver the photocopied sheets to the university for binding. Coming out of the printing office I dropped them on the muddy floor! Luckily, no real damage was done. Two weeks later my four bound copies, with the title in gold lettering along the spine, were ready for collection; one for the University library, one for the Behaviour in Organisations department, and two to place on my own bookshelves.

I deposited two of the copies with the departmental office for my examiners' assessment, and returned home in a thoughtful mood to await my fate. My work was finished; there was nothing more I could do. These two copies of my 'masterpiece', *An Organisational Study of an Ecumenical Association of Churches,* are now on the shelves of the University library, waiting to be read. I wonder if they ever will be?

20

The final hurdle to be overcome, before I was awarded my degree, came when I was called before the examiners in September 1983. This was the culmination of my four-year effort. Naturally, I was even more nervous now than I had been four years previously, as I waited in that familiar corner close to the professor's room. As I sat waiting, surrounded by all the miscellaneous notices on the walls, which had become so familiar to me from Nancey's descriptions, I hoped that this would really be my final visit to this spot.

It was by no means a foregone conclusion that I would emerge successfully from the professor's inner sanctum with the prize for which I had been striving, even though I had done everything expected of me to the satisfaction of my supervisors. Outwardly I might have appeared cool and unconcerned, but inwardly I was knotted with nerves as I went in to face my examiners. There before me were Dr Bob Cooper, my internal examiner, the external examiner, together with Professor Sylvia Shimmin. They had had my thesis for more than a month in order to scrutinise every detail for flaws and inconsistencies.

Now came the time to answer all the questions which my thesis raised. The interview continued for the best part of an hour as they went through my work with a fine tooth-comb, shooting probing questions at me. At the end of this session I felt as a professional prize fighter must feel after 15 gruelling rounds in the ring.

Suddenly, the atmosphere, which to me had seemed impersonal and tense throughout the questioning, changed as if at a given signal. The tension suddenly evaporated like the morning mist in sunlight. Both men came across the room to congratulate me. The examination was over, and I was shaken by the hand and welcomed as a Master of the University of Lancaster. Dr Cooper, who had been one of my severest critics during the previous four years, especially whilst he was my personal supervisor, was fulsome with his congratulations. Professor Shimmin, my main supervisor, was also congratulated by the examiners; I uttered an audible sigh of relief!

As I went out into the corridor Nancey came to meet me from her corner seat in the waiting area. Before I even spoke, she realised from my broad grin that the outcome of this final test was in my favour. With the ordeal behind me, I began to unwind. We headed for the campus snack bar and rehashed the doings of the previous hour over a pot of tea and a meat pie.

Getting back to a normal life after ten years' concentrated study took some doing. It was another three months before the presentation of my award in the Great Hall of the University. I was still recovering from the stress of my final examination, when I was caught up in the trappings of the academic splendour of the degree ceremony. It was a great occasion, one of the most exciting days of my life, and I meant to make the most of it. I got tickets for Paul and Susan, our son and daughter, to make it a family affair. They themselves had not done too badly academically and professionally; now it was father's turn!

Before the main ceremony I was presented to Princess Alexandra, the Chancellor of the University. For me, this brief discussion with Her Royal Highness is the most memorable part of the proceedings. Princess Alexandra is not only Chancellor of Lancaster University, she is also Colonel-in-Chief of my old regiment, The King's Own Royal Border Regiment, which made it an extra special occasion for me. This regiment is the postwar amalgamation of The King's Own Royal Regiment, and The Border Regiment – I served with both of them.

Princess Alexandra spotted my orange and gold regimental tie immediately and mentioned that she had recently returned from visiting the serving battalion of the Regiment in Germany, and could tell me that they were 'all in good heart'. This little incident was caught by the *Lancashire Evening Post* photographer. As he was doing so, part of his camera equipment embarrassingly clattered to the ground – a misfortune for him but the result was a permanent record of my meeting with the Princess, with Nancey standing close by. Before Her Royal Highness left for the robing room she said, 'I think we are all getting ready for something to eat.' She also had something to say later when I was presented on the platform.

As the family gathered with the other members of the large assembly in the Great Hall awaiting the arrival of the symbolic procession, I believe that, they too, captured something of the dignified atmosphere of the robed academics and graduates, as they shared in the recognition of my own academic achievement.

I felt strange in academic dress, complete with mortarboard, but it is not an unpleasant memory. At the age of 61, I was probably the oldest person to be getting a higher degree that year, but among the distinguished personalities receiving an Honorary Doctorate was Fenner Brockway, the veteran politician and social reformer, who was then well past his 90th year, so I considered myself in very good company.

Ceremonies and processions of this kind do not do much for me, but this had to be one of the exceptions. It was arranged that Dr Reynolds, the Vice-chancellor, in his distinctive red robe, should escort me through the platform presentation. Again, it had been requested that graduates should not be applauded individually. This custom was recognised until it was my turn to be acknowledged by the Princess, when there was a spontaneous burst of clapping from every part of the auditorium. As I lowered my head in a bow towards Princess Alexandra she said in a low voice, 'Now your wife can have a good look at you.' I was too overawed at that moment to react with anything more than a faint smile of acknowledgement. It was only afterwards when Nancey was describing what had happened that I realised that this special applause was for me. It was almost a repetition of the occasion in the Manchester Free Trade Hall when I got my first degree from the Open University.

I now had one of the qualifications I would like to have had when I was much younger, and whilst I was still available to a prospective employer, but now, that was 'water under the bridge'. My motivation for attempting these higher educational goals, in the first place, was to prove to myself and those around me that I was just an ordinary person, who, given the breaks, could prove himself capable of assimilating knowledge and applying it to good effect. There was some satisfaction in knowing that I had managed to scale some of the academic heights that once seemed out of my reach, especially when the odds were loaded against me from the start. There was nothing else for me to do but to carry on as before, using what talents and skills I had acquired in my voluntary occupations, wherever and whenever they were needed.

Epilogue

My book already existed in draft form before Nancey read to me *The Little Men* by Ken W Cooper, an ex-officer with 2nd battalion The Border Regiment. His account of what took place on the battlefield in January 1945 is a true and realistic picture of the battle, and confirms my story as I have told it, apart from the fact that he got my name wrong and called me Andrews, for which he apologised. My first contact with Ken Cooper was a card at Christmas 1993 when he wrote, 'I can see you leading your section forward as clear as day, and I knew that you had been found after the battle still alive.'

During the past 50 years many links with my Satpangan experience and its aftermath have been established. I receive letters and Christmas cards from men who were once my 'comrades-in-arms'. I frequently meet Arthur Smith from the nearby village of Croston, the Company Runner, and Eddie Hampson, from Wigan, the stretcher-bearer who lifted me from the battlefield. Last year Nancey and I revisited St Hugh's in Oxford and I was reminded of my early convalescence on my return from the Far East, as we trod the familiar corridors.

It was 30 years after Satpangan, by a strange coincidence that I met the man who picked me up from the battlefield. I had been invited to preach at the evening service in a small Methodist church in Wigan which I had not visited before. Chatting with the steward in the vestry, we got round to discussing our various war-time experiences. When I told him that I was severely wounded in Burma, he replied that he had recently attended a Burma Star Reunion as the guest of a friend. He was not sure in which unit his friend had served, but he thought that he might be present in church that night. He left the vestry and returned shortly with a man, who he introduced to me as Eddie Hampson. As we talked together we discovered that we had both been in the 2nd Borders, although Eddie was with B Company while I was with D Company. I mentioned that I lost my sight at Satpangan when I got a bullet through my head. At this Eddie said that he also had been at Satpangan, and that he was one of the stretcher-bearers. There was a pause, and after a moment he said, 'Were you that bloke we brought in after the battle – five days after being shot in the head?' 'Yes.' I said, 'that would be me!' 'Well,' he said, 'I'm the guy who picked you up!'

Many other things have happened since March 1945 when that medical orderly put the question to me, 'Would you not be better off dead than to be as you are?' At that moment I was in no fit state to answer him, but 50 years on, for better or worse, I am still around. If I have succeeded in doing anything worthwhile with my life, the credit must be widely distributed, and not given to me alone.

There have been few material rewards for my labours: the benefits have come chiefly from the challenges themselves, and from those who know my story, and who accept me and quietly share in my success.

I am, of course, thankful that I have survived an apparently fatal injury, and still have the privilege and pleasure of serving the present generation. Through it has come a full and satisfying life, enriched with children and grandchildren. I am thankful, too, for my hands which enable me to exercise the craft of picture framing in my spare time, and for modern technology, which has given me the means to process and present the events of my life in written form.

Occasionally I raise my hands and feel the place where the Japanese sniper's bullet once penetrated, leaving me with a hole in my head.

Acknowledgements

I am indebted to a multitude of ordinary men and women who from time to time have 'loaned me the use of their eyes or their arm' to assist me over the past 55 years, and who are an integral part of this story.

There are several others, too, from whom I have gained much encouragement and technical support over the same period:

Major Ken W Cooper (Retired), author of *The Little Men* and a former battalion officer in the 2nd Border Regiment.
Mr David A Castleton, former Public Relations Officer, St Dunstan's.
Mr Brian Martland, former journalist with the *Leyland Guardian*.
Mrs Jan Sutch-Pickard, Deputy Warden, Iona Community and former Editor of *Connect*

– all of whom have read my original typescript leading to its eventual publication.

I acknowledge all reprinted photographic material from:
The Bury Times, Lancashire Evening Post and *The Leyland Guardian*.

I must also mention with deepest gratitude the surgeons, doctors, nurses and ancillary medical staff who were close to the battlefield, and in the hospitals where I was treated, including Major McGregor, RAMC, members of the Queen Alexandra's Royal Nursing Service, and other assistants in the 92 and 136 Indian-British Military Hospitals, without whose skill and care I would not have survived. I owe much, too, to St Dunstan's for my initial rehabilitation, early training and continuing care as a member of the war-blinded community.

Finally, much more credit and appreciation than I am able to express here must be attributed to my dear wife Nancey, who has shared much of the pain and pleasure of putting this work together.